REALISM AND HOPE

Ronald H. Stone

University Press
of America™

Copyright © 1976 by

University Press of America, Inc.™

4710 Auth Place, S.E., Washington D.C. 20023

ISBN: 0-8191-0128-1

Dedicated to
My Parents:

Hubert and Bernice Stone

FOREWORD

This study on political realism and Christian hope is an outgrowth
of a decade of teaching Christian ethics and politics. Students from Vassar
and Morningside Colleges, Columbia, Duquesne, Pacific Lutheran, and Pittsburgh Universities, Union and Pittsburgh Theological Seminaries will recognize themes throughout the work. A few students will recognize points on
which they forced their teacher to change his position. On some issues,
they may remember that they tried to persuade him to change his mind, but
that at this date, he still clings to his original position.

The immediate occasion for the publication of the volume is the new
curriculum of Pittsburgh Theological Seminary. Reflected in these pages are
the labors for courses in The Social Teachings of the Christian Churches,
Moral Issues in International Politics, and Contemporary Political Philosophy
and Christian Ethics. In this form, the book is designed for a required
course entitled Church and Society in Global Perspective. The perspective of
the book is that of a Christian citizen reflecting through his heritage on
the problems of revolution. While in the course and in the reflection of
other readers it is assumed that the perspectives of the poor engaged in revolutionary change are also needed, the book's argument itself is directed to
North American Christians.

A word of special appreciation is offered to the members of the Community of Reconciliation who have nourished my Christian faith while I have
lived in Pittsburgh. Pittsburgh Theological Seminary and the Association of
Theological Schools have generously provided the resources which have made
the study possible. To my teachers the late Reinhold Niebuhr, John C. Bennett

and Roger Shinn, I will forever be in debt. My colleague, Walter Wiest, has listened to or read most of the chapters and to his criticism I owe whatever acuteness the thinking about revolution contains. Robert Stiver's critique has improved the manuscript and to his encouragement I owe the courage to risk publication. I hope my new friend Gustavo Gutierrez will accept this volume as a contribution to our continuing quest to articulate a liberating political philosophy.

The argument of this book has been a long time in developing, and during its gestation, pieces of it have appeared in the following publications. In its present form all the previous essays have been modified. "Political Realism and Christian Ethics" in _Religion in Life_, XXIV (Autumn, 1965), pp. 573-587; "Power and Purpose" in _Social Action_, XXIV (January, 1968), pp. 15-23; "Karl Marx and the End of Religion" in _Social Action_, XXV (November, 1968), pp. 26-39; "The Politics of the Kingdom of God" in _Christian Century_, LXXXVIII (March 17, 1971), pp. 337-340; "The Realists and Their Critics" in _Worldview_, XVI (June, 1973), pp. 19-23. The generosity of the editors of those publications who retain the copyrights, permitting the use of these materials, is appreciated.

TABLE OF CONTENTS

I. REALISM AND HOPE

The political societies in which humanity exists express the ambiguity of the human situation. Oppression is part of the human fate. Yet mankind dreams of communities organized fairly which would allow full human potential to be realized. Political philosophy and practical politics are dominated by the pull between a realistic knowledge of the oppressive state of political organization and the hope for a better future.

The bicentennial observation of the United States of America in 1976 reflected the ambiguity. There was enthusiastic joy over what had been accomplished in 200 years and deep disappointment in the forms of political oppression seen at home and abroad in the 1960's and 70's. There was hope for change and an end to imperial-type oppression, but there was also knowledge that the United States was the center of the new industrial-democratic oppression of the late twentieth century. The ongoing rivalry with the Soviet Union meant that only limited gains in social welfare and freedom could be expected in the United States. The Communist masters of the peoples of the Soviet Union deepened traditional-Russian, oppressive imperialism and no way out of the rivalry was at hand. Realistic thinkers who accepted that politics meant the domination of some people by others found it difficult to conceive of ways to substantially improve the room for freedom in the United States because of the commitments to the perpetually armed state. So the bicentennial concluded with the political options seemingly narrowed from the more hopeful days of the 1960's and early 70's. The United States was becoming an increasingly technologically-bureaucratic state committed to a welfare-warfare stance.

1

Voices were heard from beyond the technological competition of the U.S.A. and the U.S.S.R., however. Voices of hope for justice and freedom were raised from within the poor countries of the world. The voices often expressed their hopes in the demand for liberation. The quality of the future in the U.S.A. depends in part on how North Americans will respond to these cries. The United States fought the Vietnam war and lost it trying to prove that wars of liberation could not succeed. The aftermath of the war left bitterness, inflation, and political corruption at home. Americans, because of their social-political context, are inclined to be suspicious of revolution, particularly anti-capitalist revolution. When that suspicion is joined to a rabid anti-communism and to the defense of immediate North American economic interests, it results in an automatic counterrevolutionary stance. Again the ambiguity of the American bicentennial is remembered. How could a counterrevolutionary power have adequately celebrated its revolution?

The first thesis of this book includes the assumption that the U.S.A. will not become a revolutionary actor on the international scene. Such an assumption is the inescapable conclusion of realism. The first thesis is, however, that the best interests of humanity are served if the United States abandons its cold-war policies of automatically responding to revolution in a counterrevolutionary manner. So the book is hopeful. It is a hope within limits.

Situated within the North American technological-political situation, it is not our position to pretend to be radicals. We can, however, understand our situation and out of our hope support those in more desperate situations who because of that desperation are more hopeful.

The two major philosophies of hope in the world are Christianity and Communism. The hope of this volume is grounded in Christian roots. Much of the hope of the poor of the world is grounded in variants of Marxism or Christian-Marxism. This study is not a Christian-Marxist study. There are too many deep faults in Marxist theory for it to be persuasive. But there are insights in Marxism which Christianity must hear. This study, when it uses Marxist ideas, absorbs and transforms them. Augustine absorbed and transformed the pagan philosophy of Plato. Thomas Aquinas absorbed and transformed the pagan philosophy of Aristotle. Today we can be no less bold than to absorb and transform the pagan social-philosophy of Karl Marx.

Political rhetoric encourages utopianism. Political practice encourages cynicism. Politics is too serious a matter to be left either to the cynics or to the utopians. Both, however, have illuminated aspects of politics. So, if we cannot work creatively in politics without the perspectives of the cynics and the utopians, neither can we work with the perspective of only one or the other. The mind of the cynic and that of the utopian need to be engaged so that neither can forget the contribution of the other. The absolute cynic and the absolute utopian would, of course, deny the possibility of their profiting from an engaged relationship.

This study does not seek a golden mean in a compromise position between the two absolutes, but it attempts to merge the two perspectives in a new dialectical balance. It focuses on a modified form of cynicism in politics, political realism, and considers one specific form of utopian thought, that of hope for the Kingdom of God. Political realism and the hopes for the Kingdom of God are both considered in their theological expressions because, though both traditions have secular histories, they are more profoundly true in their theological expressions. The book is a study in Christian political

philosophy. More specifically, it is an essay in constructive Christian
political philosophy for American Christians who want help in understanding
how to relate practical politics and ultimate hopes for the sake of reforming the United States.

The book will offend the cynic because it speaks frankly of values.
It assumes that most Americans possess religious and ethical values which
are of fundamental importance. It assumes that the multifaceted religious
notions which characterize the American population are wiser than those of
the cynics who criticize faith as illusion. The pure idealist, though, will
find sheer idealism attacked as potentially dangerous in public life. In a
very general way, it is helpful to think of the majority of Americans as
distinct from their Western European relatives, as noticeably more religious
and self-consciously more practical or pragmatic. The skepticism of modern
France or Italy has little place in the American scene, and the overly speculative idealism of Germany only temporarily surfaces on this side of the
Atlantic. Closest to the British in politics, the American today is still
much more moved by religious symbolism than the Englishman. The Englishman
is likely to attribute his secularism to his industrialized society. The
American, who harbors feelings of a justifiable superiority in the industrial
realm, is not that attached to secularism either.

The sixties revealed to the world the failure of American ideals on
the one hand and American practical politics on the other. Vietnam, race
relations and economic justice all were discussed in lofty ideals, but in all
three areas the ideals served as rhetoric to justify misguided and sometimes
corrupt policies. Politics freed of ideals, however, also produced a Vietnam
war without justification and resistance to racial and economic justice. The
new politics proclaimed crusades and led to Vietnam, and the old politics
reinforced the error.

It is easy to be critical of the politics of the sixties; the above criticism is made only to indicate that neither idealism nor practical politics is adequate. Critics have tended to swing back and forth; one side indicates that the trouble with the country is that politicians have no values, while the other side argues we have misguided, dangerous idealists as politicians who are not in touch with reality. A second thesis of this book is that only a critical political realism informed by a vision of hope is adequate for the crisis of our time. It assumes that hope and political realism are both present in sufficient amounts in the American public to respond to the present situation. It is intended that the argument of the volume will simply hone the tools of analysis and action which are present. The book presents a tradition of political realism and then argues how this can and must be related to the primary motif of American life, expressed as the commonwealth of men in secular terms or as the Kingdom of God in traditional religious language. Yeats entitled the poem in which he said, "The best lack all conviction, while the worst are full of passionate intensity," The Second Coming. We are not at that point, for the center has held; however, the sense of hope contained in the vision of a transformed political order as well as the norms it suggests for life are a resource which political life now demands.

The book is for the sensible American who is deeply troubled about the quagmire of our common life, who is looking for practical political guidance, who has some sense that ultimately the world is guided by a divine presence, and who is willing to be persuaded that hope and political works are connected in this world.

The United States is unsure of its purpose on the world scene. The clamor of conflicting advice from abroad adds to the confusion of dissent

from within. The debate over the direction and the instruments of U.S.
foreign policy is a matter involving the whole world. Though the country
attempts to render "a decent respect to the opinions of mankind," it dimly
senses that most of its direction must come from within. Upon the ability
of the United States to understand its role depends much of the welfare and
peace of the world.

Though the stakes are great in the debate over U.S. foreign policy,
the sophistication of the debate has been relatively low. Major figures in
the country confuse dissent with disloyalty. Cliches substitute for argument.
Agreement on controversial foreign policy issues became a test of party
loyalty, and senators were purged for failing to line up with the administration on an ever-changing policy in Southeast Asia. Parents drove children
out of their homes because of issues of foreign policy which became en-
tangled in length of hair, reforms of the schools, loyalty to the government,
and affirmation of the American system. Young people self-righteously criticized their parents' political concepts and quality of life. Universities
served as recruitment centers and training grounds for the military and were
bombed in return. Neither the administrators who sought to cooperate with
the military nor those who bombed paid much attention to the faculties, who
too late tried to reason about U.S. policy in Vietnam, Laos and Cambodia.

The rhetoric is explosive and reason scarce in the debates over
foreign policy. Foreign policy is, of course, made out of pressures and
counterpressures in the face of historical contingencies and under the most
severe limits of time. Foreign policy cannot be completely rationalized
any more than one's family life ultimately makes perfect sense. Yet, it is
possible to reason about different modes of conducting a family under the
conditions of life in late twentieth-century America. Likewise, it is

possible to decry the failure of the present turmoil in foreign policy and to argue for a transformation of U.S. foreign policy with a degree of consistency and cogency.

It is a further thesis of this study that the debate over foreign policy requires that the participants in the argument possess a theoretical or philosophical understanding of the role of the U.S. in the world. Ultimately, the shape of foreign policy will be determined by politics, both domestic and international. The discussion of foreign policy and the choosing of alternative goals and alternative policies require, if they are to be undertaken wisely, a view of the whole process.

The thesis is not a twentieth-century version of Plato's argument for philosopher-kings. Statesmen do not have to be philosophers, but they must be able to understand political philosophers and to mesh their theoretical insights with the contingencies of the moment. They must, to a degree and with the aid of the philosopher, be able to grasp how the contingency of the moment relates to the whole drama of man's life in a world torn by international conflict. Happily, some of our statesmen will be philosophers, hopefully, many of them will be wise politicians. If we are fortunate, they will welcome and not fear the continuing debate over foreign policy. If a workable U.S. policy is to be set, they will participate in the debate and demand that it not be confined to ad hoc questions of present decision making.

The debate over U.S. policy is understood to include questions of both empirical and normative judgments. At stake is not only how American society does behave on the international scene, but also how it ought to behave. The questions cannot be confined to any realm of a "pure" social science, nor dare they be thought of in terms of pure intellectual theorizing. The questions of the debate are of a practical sort, and they require a practical philosophy. Political philosophy is a practical philosophy; it is neither analytical-language philosophy nor science. It may use both, but it engages in the debate as to what models of political action should be adopted by a society. The normative questions are as important as the empirical or analytical ones. "What ought the United States policy be vis-à-vis revolutionary movements?" is the type of question which cannot avoid the discourse of political philosophy.

Another thesis of the book is that, of the political philosophies which have evolved to the position where they might be regarded as schools of thought, realism is the most adequate for our times. The realism discussed here is not a static fixed philosophy but one which continues to evolve, with certain themes, convictions, and interests. The tradition of realism needs to look again at the resources in Marxist thought. It must come into contact more directly with the revolutionary movements of our times. It should continue to attempt to refine its central concepts, such as power. Realism needs to make as explicit as it can the hopes it has for the world and man's political life. The reforming drives of the realists always had within them assumptions about real gains that could be made, but their hopes were more often implicit than clearly stated. Chapters within this book begin the revision that the tradition of realism requires.

The blurring of the distinction between political philosophy and Christian social ethics is inevitable for one who is seized by the claims of the Christian faith for the clue to the ultimate human meaning of the universe. Political philosophy deals with Christian social ethics in most of its history in the West. Christian social ethics in the contemporary world utilizes the work of political philosophers, be they Christian or Jewish or Hindu.

The book lays claim to Christian realism, not just realism, because the ultimate values of the West are so thoroughly intertwined in Christian faith and culture. For the Western world there is no escape from Christianity. In either its thesis, antithesis or synthesis, political thought in the West expressed Christianity in some form. The claim means more, though, than that some theologians have contributed mightily to the emergence of this school in the last forty years in this country. Famous realists like Machiavelli and Hobbes have, perhaps, in some of their thought tried to escape Christianity. Insofar as the political philosophy here is Christian realism, it depends more on Augustine than it does on Machiavelli, and more on Calvin than on Hobbes.

Something new is happening in Western culture. Humanity is taking over more and more of its own destiny as it stands on the brink of self-destruction. Many, sensing man's new freedom and assertiveness, have celebrated the arrival of a secular age. The celebration is premature and unwarranted. The signs of religious ecstasy are as evident as the signs of secularization among the young. If mankind is on a new threshold of consciousness, it is as likely to be a breakthrough into a religiously sensitive age as it is into a sterile-technocratic age. In politics, realism without values is suicide. The values of Christian realism, of course, are subject to change and to the processes of debate, but the great advantage of Christian realism over a secular realism is the former's firm anchor in a vision of man as the bearer of the holy image. Christian realists are not free to do all American power permits them to do. Christian realism in this new age is not the same as Christian realism in the sixteenth or the fifth centuries, but neither is it the same as secular realism in the twentieth century. It has a vision of man and a hope for mankind which would be strange to a secular age. If the end of the twentieth century in the U.S. is to be an ever-increasing trend toward secularization, then Christian realism has little future. If, however, as seems more likely, the malaise of American life in the 1970's calls for a transformation of many directions in our society, a wise combination of political theory and Christian insights may yet prove to be not only viable but necessary.

It is not accidental that the same authors who wrote about the two greatest visions of a new political order also described the witness' martyr-dom. Socrates and Jesus both died at the hands of the political authorities for threatening the legitimacy of the political order, though on one level both acknowledged the authority which killed them. The visions of the Republic on the one hand and the Kingdom of God on the other have continued to shake claims for political legitimacy and their chances of doing so through all history seem high. It is not to equate either Jesus and Socrates or the Kingdom and the Republic that the above fact is noted. It is rather to point to the threatening possibilities as well as the guidelines for building a new order that these visions and martyrdoms are mentioned. The addition of the martyrdom of Sir Thomas More, the author of Utopia, to the roll of the visions, which though distant were too relevant, establishes one more connection between vision and practical politics.

Karl Marx did not understand very well the power of the vision of the Kingdom in the peasant revolutions of Europe. His comrade Engel's writing about these very Christian revolutionaries proved that Marx's "Religion is the opiate of the people" was not a universal principle. Marx did provide an alternative eschatology to the Christian vision, but the very success of his alternative vision rested upon its similarity to the Christian vision and upon being unleashed in culture prepared by Christianity.

The question of a Christian political philosophy today is whether the Marxist apocalypse has inevitably supplanted the Christian hope. This book argues that the Kingdom of God is still a vital part of contemporary Christian political philosophy. The hope of the Kingdom has resources which are richer for humane political thought than its major rival, that of Marxist ideology.

In other epochs the Kingdom of God has been used to buttress the claims of particular political authorities or to claim ultimacy for the church. The Kingdom has often been used as a hope which reduced the tension between the "ought" and the "is" by an escape into the future. The Kingdom has also motivated revolutions and its announcement resulted in martyrdoms. When Christian realism takes the hopes for the Kingdom seriously, it becomes re-vitalized so that while dealing responsibly with American power it does not sanctify that power. The Kingdom in the hands of many is a weapon against United States hegemony. The Kingdom as a source of hope for Americans and a critical norm of American pretensions reminds Americans that, though they do not have the Kingdom, there can be a place for them in a changed world. The model of the Kingdom perceived by Americans with power cannot be exactly the same model as perceived by the poor who are grasping for power. However, as Americans realize they cannot be King in the Kingdom of God, the chance for their granting citizenship to their poor brothers and sisters is enhanced. In the forging of the claims of the Kingdom and the political knowledge of the realists a way of combining theory and practice, hope and action can be found.

II. THE KINGDOM OF GOD AS A POLITICAL MODEL OF HOPE

Once again the theological mood of the American churches is shifting as they struggle to find a new model for the Christian life. As in every past epoch of the churches' life, they have had to rethink and articulate their response to their God in terms of the culture in which they were living, so the present crises force that rethinking of their symbols. The disarray in the churches' thought is obvious; the emerging shape of their action is not so clear. Yet, the Christian tradition offers a model which can adequately express the new forces pulsing in their life. And, just as revolutions in society are stimulated by reaching back to purer patterns of life and thought, so the revolution in the church waits upon the rediscovery of the model contained in its origins.

As history reveals, the patterns of social ethics and the theologies which inform those ethics are not so often refuted as laid aside by the church. For instance, Karl Barth's theology has not been decisively disproven, but it no longer claims the interest of very many theologians. And, the social gospel movement was not routed in formal argument; rather, in responding to new problems, its leaders articulated new models of understanding. Social forces in and outside the church combined to usurp part of the movement's program and to render other parts irrelevant. Or again, the rebuttal to the "death of God" theology was not so brilliant as to dispose of it intellectually; rather, the failure of proponents of that theology to find ways of meeting the religious needs of twentieth century man doomed their ideas. Which is to say that prevailing patterns of thought in theology and ethics are disavowed when they can no longer handle pressing contemporary problems.

12

This is a process observable in other fields also. Thus, Thomas S.
Kuhn argues, in The Structure of Scientific Revolutions,[1] that fundamental
changes in scientific thinking occur when the established paradigms, or accepted models and patterns, no longer function adequately. At the turn of
the fifteenth century, Ptolemaic astronomy had developed to the point where
it was unworkable. It was producing a picture of a very untidy world. So
it was replaced by Copernican astronomy. Reinforcing this technical shift
were social pressure for calendar reform and changes in metaphysical assumptions. Nevertheless, the shift did not come without struggle. To suggest
that the prevailing models have outlived their usefulness is always risky.

It is especially risky in theology. For who can be sure there?
Change might be a blind alley or a repetition of the mistakes of the past.
Normally, in theological understanding gains are made by the continued
refining of questions and historical research within the ruling patterns of
thought. Today, however, it appears that the widespread dissatisfaction in
the church may be a prelude to change.

Many voices are demanding that the churches adopt new ways of thinking about their social responsibility and the theological expression thereof.
The theology of hope--particularly as set forth in Jurgen Moltmann's Religion,
Revolution and the Future[2] and Rubem Alves' A Theology of Human Hope[3]--holds
that the prevailing Christian social ethic has failed because it despairs of
this world and leaves men only with otherworldly hopes that are irrelevant to
the revolutionary task here on earth. Moltmann would have Christians root
their political hopes in the resurrection of Christ. But resurrection, however we affirm it, cannot be affirmed as a normal event. And, indeed, Alves
criticizes Moltmann for not grounding his analysis securely enough in human
history. Yet, like Moltmann, he fails to deal seriously with the stuff of

history. Both these theologians see revolution in a romantic glow, but they take no account of what actually happened in the revolutions of modern times, from the American to the Russian, the Mexican to the Chinese, the French to the Algerian. At least in the books cited above, they are innocent of political philosophy, political history and the sociology of politics (save for a few references to Marx--and usually to the young humanist Marx).

On the other hand, the theologians of the counter-culture probably break with the tradition of Christian social ethics which limited itself to trying to advise the establishment. Both Harvey Cox (The Feast of Fools[4]) and Michael Novak (A Theology for Radical Politics[5]) insist that a new ethic is being born in the various counter-cultures and that the church must espouse it as far as it is valid and criticize it so far as it is inadequate. But rather than suggesting new paradigms for the church's future work, these two volumes reveal the quixotic nature of the counter-cultures they celebrate.

More persuasive is James Cone in his Black Theology and Black Power.[6] Cone demonstrates the absolute priority of bringing together the movement for justice and an adequate theology for black men. While he fails in his attempt to identify blackness with the universalism of the church, he takes us a long way toward a sound theology for liberation. Indeed, this book evidences a theological tension and growth toward a new model on the part of its author who, while himself citing Barth and Bonhoeffer to support his ideas, criticizes Americans for depending on European theology. A Black Theology of Liberation[7] pushes the dualism of black and white to an ontological level. Despite the power and beauty of his writing and genuine helpfulness in church-society tactics, this continuing dualism (should one say Manichaeanism?) reduces the value of his study particularly for non-black populations or Christian churches who are tired of over-simple dichotomies.

Historical research also has led many to push for changes in the church's understanding of itself vis-à-vis society. There has been a rediscovery of the church's radical politics at various times in the past. Michael Walzer's The Revolution of the Saints[8] stresses the revolutionary role of English Puritanism in the seventeenth century, and the late Reinhold Niebuhr praised the Puritan experiment as the most creative period in Christian social philosophy. Certainly they are on the right track. Hitherto many forces have conspired to obscure the Christian faith's resources for fostering thoroughgoing social reformation. The historian's task is now to find out which of them the churches in fact made use of. He will, for instance, have to reassess the various Anabaptist revolts which the mainline reformers helped to crush. And Martin Luther's divorce between the freedom of Christian man and the need of the Christian man to be liberated from social and economic oppression will not withstand the scrutiny of historians of doctrine in touch with today's world.

Biblical scholarship confronts us with a plurality of responses in The New Testament to questions about the political order and also about the Kingdom of God. The contrast in the attitude of the state in Romans 13 and Revelation 13 is striking. Similarly the references to the Kingdom of God within the synoptic gospels are not all easily reconciled to each other or to the Fourth Gospel. Revelation again contrasts with the Pauline teaching slightly by suggesting a co-reigning of Christ and God rather than Paul's vision of Christ delivering the Kingdom of God. The passages in the synoptics portray both an imminent Kingdom and a present Kingdom. Some references present the Kingdom as a coming crisis, probably in the near future; another group of teachings emphasizes the organic growth aspects of the Kingdom followed by a consummation. The purpose here is not to sort out a thesis as to the predominant New Testament perspective on the Kingdom of God or the political order, but only to indicate that the plurality of responses frees Christians to consider anew a theological understanding of their hopes. The canon itself, in its diversity, provides the argument for freedom to think through the meaning of the Kingdom for our time.

Yet the church today finds it harder to distinguish itself from the culture. Powerful forces like those represented by former Vice-President Agnew and former President Nixon took the church to task whenever she seemed to be critical of American life. President Nixon's public piety reminded us of the Constantinian era when Caesar and the church were yoked together. How doubt Caesar if he appears with Billy Graham in a mass rally? Heavily secularized as they are, the churches do not know where to look for their distinctiveness. Like Mary at the tomb they are driven to cry, "They have taken away my Lord and I do not know where they have laid him." The churches feel the burden of public despair pushing down upon them. The people are well aware that our institutions are not working but feel powerless to renew either the institutions or themselves. Where can hope come from if not from the church?

Her leadership must find a direct way to counter the attacks of conservatives who deny that she has any message for society. Where, they ask, do you root the social message you preach? Often that question is raised in bad faith. Sometimes, though, it is raised out of anguish. Many a conservative Christian would accept the social implications of the faith if a clear theological case for social responsibility were presented to him.

More frightening is the movement of reaction which is spreading across the country. Clergy and laity alike feel the pressures of the politics of fear. Where are they going to find resources to cope with the forces

of prejudice and greed? Surely in a new model for understanding the relationship of the church to society--a model incorporating a vision broad enough
to inspire the rebellious young to turn toward the faith. At the same time
it must be a social model (for most of our problems are caused by a brutal
misconception of individualism) grounded in a hope that will overcome despair
while not feeding illusions. Again, it must be a model that allows Christians
to distinguish themselves from the culture even while driving them to be
responsible in society. Finally, it must be a model rooted in the Christian
tradition. Though that tradition is very pluralistic, a model that broke
with it radically would have little chance with the mass of Christians. The
ultimate test of any paradigm for Christian social existence is, of course,
ethical: "You will recognize them by the fruits they bear."

The ethos of despair, the confusion in the local congregations, and
the direction of the newer theologies all point toward the need for a new
pattern of understanding. The pattern needed has been suppressed for fifty
years. Just as it was rediscovered in the closing years of the nineteenth
century, so it needs to be recovered again. The model that is called for is
the Kingdom of God. Men desperately need a confidence that the vision of the
prophets and the hope of Jesus are going to be realized. The Kingdom is, of
course, the eternal rule of God in all ages and places. It is also the unique
relationship that faithful Hebrews and Christians feel as they accept citizenship in the Kingdom. It is fundamentally for our time the hope that people
will in the future be freed from oppression to the liberty of love in a
commonwealth governed by the only power which can fulfill the needs of mankind. Wolfhart Pannenberg has called the Kingdom of God "that perfect society
of men which is to be realized in history by God himself."[9]

The synoptic gospels portray Jesus as the announcer of the Kingdom of God. Jesus announces, repent because of the good news of the arrival of the Kingdom. The Kingdom is the message most often on his lips. His ministry, his parables, his ethics, and his death are all intelligible only in the light of his focus on the Kingdom.

The Romans who put the inscription "The King of the Jews" on his cross combined understanding with confusion. He was not a zealot, but he did proclaim a new order which many confused with violent revolution and which, more importantly, subverted the piety and civic religion of Rome. His proclaimed Kingdom was more radical than the goals of the zealots because it went to the root of humanity's social existence and would shake the prideful structures of men forever.

Careful study of his parables reveals that he thought of the Kingdom as combining the eternal rule of God with the coming messianic theocracy. The structure of life is hidden, but the violation of it leaves humanity distraught and oppressed. He thought of it as expressing the special relationship of Israel to its Lord. Kings reigned in Israel but when they knew what they were about they ruled in the midst of the tension that characterized Israel. I Samuel 8 established the pattern of kingship in Israel as one in tension with the more fundamental rule of Yahweh. Israel served within God's Kingdom with a rigor that was not expected of the nations. Jesus also understood the Kingdom as a new rule of God over the hearts and actions of persons in a transformed age. He probably thought that that age was coming soon. Paul thought the Kingdom was coming soon in his early ministry; later he adjusted his expectations to the delayed parousia.

The late H. Richard Niebuhr caught a redeeming feature of American Christianity when he argued that its central theme was the Kingdom of God.[10]

He also emphasized that, though various movements of Christians and theologians interpreted the Kingdom differently, there were three major strands
which reinforced each other: the Kingdom as the will of God expressed in His
dominion over life; as the rule of God in Christ in the individual mind or
soul of the faithful; and as the coming consummation of God's rule over His
commonwealth. Each theme needed the support of the others, and each was
subject to the eroding forces of secularism in his day.

Today the coming Kingdom of God is a religiously affirmed hope that
frees one from lesser utopian schemes and provides the courage for shoulder-
ing the tasks of responsible life now. People will not build it in their
own prideful autonomy, but neither are their strivings irrelevant to its
approach.

The Kingdom of God is a vision rested in a hope that God's righteousness will prevail. It is a social model of God's new action. In the present
we all serve in God's Kingdom in the midst of other relative kingdoms. We
seek both the ultimate peace of God and the peace of our earthly kingdoms.
We hope in a coming Kingdom, the shape of which we cannot predict. This
hope makes sense out of the radicalness of our concerns today because we
know that ultimately love will out in its own way. The way may be through
convulsion and strange reversals of our social life, but ultimately God will
prevail. We trust this in faith as we trust that He saved, on the edge of
the void, Christ from meaninglessness.

The Kingdom is not to be equated with a one person/one vote uni-
cameral legislature for the whole world, nor with other schemes be they
integration, socialism, or world federalism. The structures of the Kingdom
are not clear. On Jesus' authority the vision includes happiness for those
who have been oppressed, fullness for the seekers of righteousness,

blessedness for the peacemakers, a place for those who have been persecuted, a reward for the meek and merciful. The hope of the great reversal promises justice for those who have benefited from unjust structures and redress to those who have suffered from misallocated powers. The very generalness of the Kingdom is a necessary feature of the vision. If the Kingdom were expressed in particular detail, strivers would either become fanatical in trying to realize particular social reforms through power politics or in obtaining some feature they would become self-righteous in thinking they had arrived.

The Kingdom of God is the Christian's expression of social hope. It is the protest against the reality of oppression and the promise of a new order. It wells up within human nature as the theological expression of rule without oppression where God the creator rules through humanity realizing love and justice.

The Kingdom has been delayed, or at least it has not come as soon as some passages in The New Testament implied. That is a more serious problem for those passages in The New Testament than it is for us. Humanity cannot give up hope, for to do so would leave it living in a world where the mythology of death prevailed. It dare not abandon the Kingdom for an otherworldly view of heaven, for to do so robs its struggles for a more just society of meaning.

The model of the Kingdom contains the cry of the oppressed of the world for justice and for a world in which one can love. Abandoning the Kingdom for cynical politics or for otherworldly hopes cuts the union between the good news of the gospel and the liberation of people. The Kingdom is not the opiate of the people, but the model of what human life is meant to be. The trust in its coming is our hope, the living of its ethic in a world not ready for it is the strange joy and responsibility of Christians.

Christian life is to be lived in terms of the politics appropriate to the Kingdom of God. The movement of the Kingdom is focused in Jesus, and in his life and death, and through the ministry of Paul the Kingdom is opened to gentiles. Israel and the New Israel constitute earthly representations of the future Kingdom and embody the message of the coming Kingdom. Christians must live within the ultimate structures of the world, as citizens of the church and according to a style suitable to the coming fulfillment of the Kingdom. They serve the King in a realm in which his rule is incomplete. Many courses of action are clear for Christians; they must contend against structures which stand in contradiction to the arrival of the Kingdom. Prisons which fail to reform, governments which govern unjustly, and prejudices which reinforce bigotry must be eliminated. Efforts toward liberation of people, development of community, and achievement of equality must be supported, for these have a place in the coming Kingdom.

The Kingdom is a hope. Though it can be neither verified nor falsified in the present, it contains assurance of future verification. The Kingdom is felt as a present need, and it pulls together the expressions of a broken culture and a searching church. Alternatives to the Kingdom seem pale by comparison; they lead to secular fanaticisms or otherworldly illusions. The best evidence for the adequacy of the Kingdom is the quality of the lives that are produced in the living out of citizenship in it.

III. CHRISTIAN FAITH AND REVOLUTION

The faith of Christians has been condemned as an opiate which hides
the pain of alienation from men and women and consequently prevents them from
becoming revolutionaries. Alternatively the faith has been criticized for
being fundamentally a disquieting force which inclines people to revolutionary
activity. In an age of vast, rapid, social, technological and ideological
change it is nearly imperative that Christians inquire as to the relationship
of their faith to the change which is transforming humanity in fundamental
ways. Debates as to the contemporary church's role in revolutionary activity
are generally inconclusive. There is very little secure ground on which to
stand to observe the present turmoil in society and the church. In any case,
an adequate answer to inquiries regarding the relationship between Christian
faith and revolution will not be found by appealing either to the martyred,
revolutionary priests or to the other Christians who helped hunt them down.
Our inquiry into the meaning of Christian faith in revolutions must be more
fundamental than a contemporary sociological head-count of what Christians in
fact do.

The question about the relationship of revolution and Christian faith
is not to be answered by polling Christians, be they Americans or Cubans.
The question cannot be answered, either, by reference exclusively to The New
Testament, for there the faith is located in one complex of political loyalties and one historical epoch.

Moltmann is certainly correct when he argues that the turmoil that
early Christians caused in the sacral-political mythos of their day threatened
to undermine the legitimacy of contemporary authority.[1] It takes a hermeneutic

22

already committed to the values of humanistic revolution, however, to find
in The New Testament much of what common discourse regards as political revolutionary rhetoric or action. Pieces are there, and a new vision is certainly
present, but despite the major motifs of the redefinition of eschatological
messianism, The New Testament in some fundamental ways is beyond politics
while still quite historical. Moltmann uses the term politics very loosely,
and the disagreement with him is in part a matter of definition. However,
beyond the differences in definition, the following claim seems exaggerated:

> Yet through their worship of God in the crucified Jesus,
> the Christians were certainly acting as revolutionaries.
> For by so doing they seized the nerve-center of the
> political religions and the religious politics of their
> time.[2]

Seizing the "nerve-center" sounds much more like what the Bolsheviks did when
they put down the Orthodox Church and murdered the czar and his family than
like the disengaged attitude of the early church from the Roman empire. The
early Christians had very little sense of attacking directly the distribution
of power in the Roman empire.

Revolution can be thought of as a transformation of a people's life,
including their economics, politics, morals and religion. The revolution is
completed only when the old rules, system, and principles of legitimacy have
been overthrown and replaced by that alternative which previously was suspect,
heretical, or illegal. Times of revolution are times when people change
their self-consciousness and experience themselves and their worlds differently. Perceiving revolution in this way might lead one to say that the
early Christians were radically changing the terms of their existence but the
massive social structures of their empire were affected only slightly.

The good news of the coming Kingdom is in essence a liberating force;
it will and does have revolutionary consequences. However, in this history

no political solution will ultimately liberate humanity, and our truest
liberty comes in knowing both the limits of history and our own freedom in
Christ. The revolutionary potential of the gospel for politics is not
obvious. Because Luke 4:18-19 is not for one revolution only but for the
continued struggle of people who bear the name of the crucified one, it does
not say you must be at this particular place in this particular revolution.

> The Spirit of the Lord is upon me, because he has anointed
> me to preach good news to the poor. He has sent me to
> proclaim release to the captives and recovering of sight
> to the blind, to set at liberty those who are oppressed,
> to proclaim the acceptable year of the Lord.

Jesus as Revolutionary

Current scholarship, life styles and issues have created a fascination for the quest of the historical Jesus' stance regarding revolution.
This brief discussion will not try to replace the recent valuable studies of
John Yoder, George R. Edwards, S. G. F. Brandon and Oscar Cullmann. It suggests an interpretation of the politics of the last week of Jesus' life with
which probably all four of the authors would agree, despite their continuing
disagreements with each other. The position of Brandon in itself is not
reconcilable with the positions of Yoder, Edwards and Cullmann.

This subject is primarily a search growing out of the fact that in
the jungles of the tropics and in the universities of the United States
decisions are made which use an image of Jesus for motivation or rationali-
zation. Dictators paraphrase his words on their self-deifying statues, and
children abandon their bourgeois homes to follow a message they attribute
to him. Seminarians demonstrated against the Vietnam war carrying a huge
wooden cross, while inside the White House a pious President consulted with
clergy who, serving in Jesus' name, disagreed with the seminarians' goals.

In a secularized world maybe the understanding of what happened in Jerusalem would not be important, but in the world in which we live the understanding of his last week is vitally important.

The Old Testament, over seventy-five per cent of the Christian's Bible, is replete with political theology. The Old Testament is a history of tribulation and conflict in which Israel's faith and nationhood begin in a slave revolt. Moses, a murderer of an Egyptian officer, leads a revolt that disrupts Egypt's plans for city building. In the contest between the slaves and the oppressor, the Hebrew God vanquishes Pharoah, who is also a god. The destruction of Pharoah and his army liberates Israel and casts the tribes into their long struggle with the Canaanite peoples for a homeland.

The political theology of The Old Testament binds their God into a political treaty with his people. This covenant becomes the focus of their religious-political understanding. In their search for security, the people forget their dependence on the mysterious God of the exile and forge strange alliances and worship other deities. Again and again they forget the nature of justice presupposed in their religion and adopt the more oppressive ways of the social systems which surround them.

When Israel becomes a monarchy, the loyalty due to the King is qualified. The prophets remain God's spokesmen, and they fulfill that role by reminding the King that he is not divine but human and that he is subject to criticism. Even so, the monarchy is too proud to sustain itself, and God and his prophets are involved in destroying the united monarchy and dividing the tribes into two countries.

The political theology of The Old Testament is particularly evident in Samuel I and II and Kings I and II. The stories are of the religious conflicts of the priests and prophets being plowed into the soil of Israel's history. Slowly standards of justice are elaborated and violated. Revolutions and wars come and pass, and they are all loaded with religious meaning.

The Old Testament is the tale of a God seeking true worship and a just order for a people whose identity depends upon their covenant together. The books of their law, of their literature, and of their prophets never stray far from the central issues of their political theology. The question to be asked is: Does the political theological interest of The Old Testament continue in The New Testament? The answer is, yes, but with the understanding that whereas God had been understood as governing a particular kingdom, now he is seen as transforming the history of that kingdom into the salvation of the whole world. The focus of The New Testament is on the emergence of the church which will deplace the old historical kingdom as the center of God's work with the hope of a coming Kingdom. The political-theological focus continues, but with the differences demanded by the gospel being released to the world. The story is now written in Greek for all of the Hellenistic world and not in Hebrew for a small people.

According to the first chapter of The New Testament, Jesus is a descendant of kings, though born lowly. His very birth is a threat to the state, which is portrayed in the re-enactment of the murder of the innocents which had accompanied Moses' birth. Jesus himself begins life as a political exile in Egypt. The King Herod and the Emperor Caesar both leave the imprint of their presence and their policies upon the early New Testament chapters.

John the Baptist, who ordains Jesus, is killed by the political authorities for challenging the prerogatives of the royal family. The Devil tempts Jesus to practice magic and to worship him, promising him bread, power over gravity and political power if he will only serve the Prince of Evil.

Jesus does not reject gravity, bread or political power, but neither will he turn from his mission or his ultimate loyalty to pursue them.

The drama of The New Testament is played out against the background of a fanatical Jewish revolt against Rome. Every religious group is marked strongly by its attitude toward Rome as by its distinctive doctrinal position. After Jesus, Rome at first tolerates Christians as a Jewish sect, and Paul can appreciate Rome's benevolent order and perceive it as expressing God's ordering plan. Then Rome turns to persecute the church, and the author of Revelation portrays Rome not benevolently but as a beast demanding idolatry. The beast will be destroyed by both worldly and supernatural powers. Jesus' message of the coming Kingdom of God was preached in a world where the many conflicts over the order of the kingdom were daily fare for the population and their imperial rulers.

A warning must be made. The argument is not that The New Testament is a treatise in political philosophy, even though most of the political philosophy of the Western world has made very heavy use of it until quite recently. The political context of The New Testament is important, though, and there are political theologies there for those who will patiently seek them. Twentieth-century readers must avoid reading themselves into first-century conflicts, but for Christians the message of The New Testament is too important for them to remain ignorant of its political implications.

The political theology of The New Testament is found primarily in the events of Holy Week. The gospels are written with Holy Week as their focus. They are a new form of literature in which the tragedy is overcome by resurrection, and the whole story is told in that light. All the sayings of Jesus, the letters of Paul, the apocalyptic literature of John must be interpreted from the facts of Holy Week and the faith of Easter.

Probably, "The most certain thing known about Jesus of Nazareth is
that he was crucified by the Romans as a rebel against their government in
Judaea."[3] The gospels and the Roman historian Tacitus agree on this point.
Josephus records the crucifixion of many Jewish rebels during this period.
The question, of course, arises as to whether or not he was innocent of the
crime for which he was put to death. The gospels regard him as innocent.
Some contemporary interpreters, notably Brandon, regard him as guilty and
think that the gospel writers had to hide this guilt to make the new, weak
community of Christians appear acceptable to the Roman world. Oscar Cullmann,
in Jesus and the Revolutionaries,[4] takes the opposing position that Jesus was
not a revolutionary.

According to the gospels, the Romans treated Jesus as if he were a
rebel. They mocked him as a pretender to the throne. They published a claim
to be the "King of the Jews" in Aramaic, Greek and Latin on his cross, as if
that claim were the reason for his state execution. The gospel writers portray Pilate as willing to release Jesus or Barabbas, a Zealot leader caught
in the recent insurrection in Jerusalem. The Zealots also taught a doctrine
of a future Kingdom of God, but equated such a Kingdom with a revived Jewish
monarchy governing Jerusalem. Jesus was executed between two men referred
to by a Greek term which can be translated equally well as either criminal or
rebel. At the time of the week's events, Jerusalem and Judaea were seething
with revolt. Jesus entering Jerusalem in such a time, with Zealots among his
band of followers and in a manner evoking Messianic claims, could not avoid
being seen as a threat to the system. Jesus probably was suspected of being
a Zealot; at least his political loyalties were repeatedly at issue, and he
did not attack the Zealot movement.

Significant to an interpretation of Jesus' actions is the disruption of the Temple. He seems to have been at the Temple continually for several days. There for a week he taught and attacked the system of the Temple at its vulnerable point, its economy. The Temple authorities desired to arrest him, but they could not because of the crowd. "But when they tried to arrest him, they feared the multitudes." The Temple authorities were collaborators with the imperial power, and their prestige was dealt a harsh blow by their inability to deal with this teacher in their own precinct.

Every society is held together by understandings which are grounded in each society's deepest assumptions about humanity and god. These understandings were incarnated in the Temple authorities' collaboration with Rome and their resulting privileges. Brandon reminds us that, when the Zealots revolted years later, one of their first acts was to put the temple authorities to death. Jesus was not a Zealot, nor was he pursuing political power over people, but he attacked the Roman-Jewish understandings which legitimated the status quo. By his actions he committed just what the gospels portray his critics of accusing him of: blasphemy and sedition. Jesus' activities were clearly blasphemous and seditious according to the canons of those in power. His confrontation with the powerful undercut the legitimacy of those standards.

Jesus did not join the violent revolutionaries. If he had, we today would question his political judgment. He seemed to know that reliance on military force was self-defeating, or so at least he has been portrayed by the gospel writers after Jerusalem was destroyed. He criticized the system at its center by disruptive actions and by teaching. He proclaimed a vision of a new order, and thus threatened all those whose loyalties were to the old order, that compromise of Judaism and Rome. When religion sanctifies bad political arrangements, those who protest what is being sanctified are dealing in both blasphemy and sedition.

In Holy Week, much of the world finds its salvation. Also to be found there is a reminder that the world does not tolerate preaching of the Kingdom of God, if it is threatened thereby. There in Jerusalem the most holy man met the most human, as expressed in a legal and religious system, and that system killed the man. The one, confessed as Lord by much of the world, was killed by the imperial power of his day in a far-off corner of its empire which it did not understand.

Today Christians are found both in the imperial powers and in those far-off corners of the empire. They are citizens both of the church and the nations. The Kingdom which Jesus preached relativizes all their governments and their churches and promises a new future.

The distance between Jesus, the disturber of Jerusalem's peace, and the resurrected Christ of the Christian community is not inconsequential. It is the difference between life and death. The Christian community found the life-renewing force of Jesus continuing in its midst and, by proclaiming his resurrection, established his eventual victory over Rome. The road was long and hard with the Christian community after Jesus, alternately rejecting and praying for the world in which it found itself. The shock of the death of Jesus was endured by resurrection faith and the shock of the delayed parousia, the Kingdom's arrival, has required a variety of adjustments through the ages. The churches have spiritualized the Kingdom, internalized the Kingdom, substituted a doctrine of heavenly immortality for the Kingdom, confused evolution with the Kingdom, and preached revolution as the Kingdom.

Throughout its history the church has shaken the world by changing its conception of the meaning of the Kingdom of God. These structures of

meaning have strengthened failing nerves as civilizations were toppling,
as did Augustine's doctrine of two cities. They have also broken the ethos
of a given civilization. The forces unleashed by Jesus have often undone
the synthesis of an empire and a culture. Three examples of a new concep-
tualization of salvation, meaning, end time and their consequences follow.
The first example is of a Papal claim to embody the Kingdom so completely
that his office should rule the world. The second is Luther's argument for
God's rule over earth being realized properly in two realms. His vision of
the Divine government threw Europe's earthly governments into conflict for
years. Finally the Calvinists of England pursued a rigorous model of trying
to base their earthly commonwealths on the Kingdom of God.

A Papal Revolution

In many of the liberal arts curriculums of our universities the
Gregorian revolution is described as a contest between church and state.
Such a labeling is confusing because in the eleventh century neither state
nor church, as we think of them, existed. It is rather that out of the
struggle for control of the unified Christian society of the eleventh century,
forces were unleashed which would contribute to the eventual establishment of
the church and states in Europe as we know them.

Hildebrand or Gregory VII (1073-1085) was a product of the Cluniac
reform movement which had already created in the Cluniac monasteries the
first transnational corporation, established a democracy in death through the
institution of All Soul's Day, and attacked various corruptions in both secular and ecclesiastical government. The papal court had been set against the
imperial palace, and events in the late tenth and early eleventh centuries
set the stage for a revolution which would strip the emperor of much of his

authority and institute radically new practices in ecclesiastical, political and philosophical life.

The content of the Gregorian revolution, according to Eugen Rosenstock-Huessy,[5] was the establishment of central ecclesiastical government in Rome by which every Christian soul gained the theoretical right of appeal to Rome. Before Gregory the bishops, usually dominated by the local government, were supreme. The papal court tore down the feudal allegiances and, in the name of universalism, established direct allegiance between each Christian and the pope.[6]

The Gregorian movement was a triumph for asceticism. As priests were to be freed from their entangling feudal responsibilities, so they were to be freed from the responsibilities of the bed of either their mistress or wife. It took fifty years to establish the rule of celibacy for the priests, and those priests and bishops who resisted were largely connected with the imperial party in the struggle between pope and emperor. The symbol of the reformed and reorganized clergy became celibacy and the pro-Roman celibate clergy took the name of "Spirituals" for themselves and the old clergy were labeled worldly or secular clergy. It was an appeal to age, to the role of the grandfather who stood beyond human passions and the clamor of the world. The priests, in a day when few lived to old age, came to represent the "third age," the age beyond the passions.[7]

Hildebrand's taking of the name of Gregory VII was in itself significant; by so doing he affirmed his loyalty to Gregory VI who had been forced out of office in 1046 by imperial action. It also indicated his dependence upon Gregory I (590-604) in thought. Other reforming popes in his tradition from 1047 to 1146 chose names from among the venerable fathers of the first centuries of the church. Here truly was a mark of "Renaissance,"[8] as popes chose to identify with earlier, purer times.

The ideology of the Gregorian revolution was thoroughgoing. The
dissolution of present historical forms was promoted by an alliance of the
future with prehistory. Tradition and custom were strong, but if they were
shown to be particular by being out of continuity with that which was coming
and the past which was conceived in universal terms, they were severely
undermined.

Anselm of Lucca was called upon to justify the overthrow of the apos-
tolic and liturgical claims of the emperor which seemed to have at least
five hundred years of historical support behind them. Anselm's words are as
bold as those of any radical today:

> You say that this execrable form of government over the
> church has lasted an immeasurable length of time, through
> all of which time the rulers of this earth had the power of
> appointing bishops. That is no argument. A perversion
> introduced by the princes of this world can be no prejudice
> to the right form of government, through whatever length of
> time it may have prevailed. Otherwise, our Lord God himself
> would be guilty, since he left mankind in bondage to the
> devil, to the deformation of true government and only redeemed
> it by his own death after the lapse of five thousand years![9]

Anselm made the wisdom of the years a perversion. The past did not sanctify.
Empires cannot be based on arguments that for five hundred years they have
maintained themselves. All of the revolutions of Europe join prehistory with
the future. The present in the eye of the revolutionary, even though it has
survived an epoch, is a perversion when viewed from prehistory and the needs
of the future.

The shifts in judging the present by the future rather than the past
were not confined to questions of church government. Humanity was coming
into a new relationship with nature in the eleventh century. The relatively
simple technological shift in the technique of harnessing horses to carts
promised to open a new era. Europe was becoming unified through the possibility of the transportation of stone as a building material. The new

harnesses made possible the construction of stone bridges and stone castles at places far removed from the supply of building materials. This in turn meant better protection, fewer armies of wandering knaves, and a sense of unification. Twelfth-century artists portrayed the church herself riding in a cart. That symbol captured the rise of the Roman church to a new position of predominance over a Europe with which she could now communicate.[10]

The papacy now wrested the figure of the wandering apostle Paul from its imperial connections and defined the city of Rome as the center of the world.[11] The crusades also enhanced the claims of the pope to be a world-wide ruler as opposed to the petty and local regimes of the secular rulers.

The greatest manifesto of the Gregorian revolution was a gift of the spirit to the pope who dictated it for his private consideration. The Dictatus Papae contains within itself the first claim for a universal revolution in Western history. Other revolutions which have contributed significantly to the mainstream of Western life have followed Gregory in claiming universality. For example he claimed:

1. The Roman church is founded by God alone.

2. Nobody except the High Priest of Rome can be named ecumenical.

8. He is the only one who shall wear imperial insignia.

9. The pope's feet all princes shall kiss.

18. He can depose emperors.

20. Nobody can judge him.[12]

Hildebrand died in exile, but his priests assured him that he could not die in exile because the earth had been given him. Forty years of struggle followed and, in 1122, a Concordat at Worms brought peace. The Concordat recognized that the radical faith of Christians may carry them into revolutionary activity and that government cannot survive if its people are ready to die for a higher legality in anti-governmental acts.

In the Concordat at Worms is anchored firmly the dualism of Western political life. Here rests Western freedom. Some type of dualism (or perhaps pluralism) is necessary for freedom. Monism in political life rushes toward despotism, and the contemporary Western political life without a divided legality finds pressures toward repressive government almost irresistible. The fight from Gregory VII's perspective was for the liberty of a reforming church, and in creating a transnational and universal church he enriched the liberty of the Western peoples. The crusades, Gothic architecture, scholasticism are involved in the mission of this papal revolution, but the purposes of this chapter do not permit pausing long enough here to develop all of these connections.

The radical shifts in eschatological thinking in the Gregorian revolution foreshadowed later shifts in Lutheran and Puritan revolutionary thinking. Civilization was so shaken by the Gregorian revolution that the emphasis shifted, at least in curialist literature, to thinking of the end of time in terms of the anti-Christ rather than the Last Judgment. The anti-Christ symbol is more worldly, more connected with this history and also more useful to the papalist party than the Last Judgment. The heavenly city had nearly been realized by the popes; the only force which could prevail against it would be the anti-Christ. As the vicar of Christ, the pope viewed history from the perspective of Christ's final judgment and could unleash actions against the very real and present anti-Christs. Any emperor who claimed connection with the final goal of history could be seen in the role of anti-Christ. As the enemies of a Marxist revolution are counter-revolutionaries, the enemies of the papalist revolution were anti-Christs and the party and the church must be ever on guard against these forces.

The church made visible the mysteries of God and looked back from
the goal of mankind to expose the enemies of the mysteries and of the goal.
Luther protested against this making visible objectification of the mysteries
and against the anticipation of the Last Judgment and the control of God's
Judgment by the church.

Luther replaced the model of the papal reformers and their successors
with the elusive, always coming, but not yet realized Kingdom of God. The
anti-Christ for Luther was in the papacy itself, which had captured and betrayed the dealings of God with humanity.

The Puritans and many left-wing sects of the Reformation felt Luther
did very little to realize the Kingdom. They wanted to create it here on
earth or at least to remove more obstacles to its coming than did the Lutherans,
who in some respects seemed to sacrifice even the gains of the Gregorian revolution.

These acts of revolutionizing the "ends of time" may seem irrelevant
or overly speculative to the contemporary "scientific" historian. But it is
out of these changes in perspective that the shaking events, which distinguish
epochs, arise. The French and Russian revolutions, no less than the Christian
revolutions discussed here, altered the end conceptions of time. Revolutionaries tend to interfere with the ways of Providence quite boldly. Whether
or not "humble revolutionary" is a contradiction in terms will remain an
open question, but it does not describe the revolutionaries we are examining.
These acts of renaming the ages or presenting new constructs of humanity's
end have little to do with ordinary politics or ordinary people, but they are
the visions out of which institutions and people die and from which are born
new institutions and new men and women. The criticism of institutions from
the perspective of how they will die is one of the most important sources of

the critical spirit in the West. The ongoing critical spirit may in fact enable them to live.

Lutheran Revolution

The study of revolution is a study in irony. Luther, believing deeply in the distance between the sacred realm and the secular realm, directed his energy to reforming the sacred realm. In the process he also revolutionized the secular realm. The man who changed Western life with his writing appears in his writing to have little interest in the change of the secular realm. The refutation of the distance between the sacred realm and the secular realm which was a key concept in his revolution lies within the influence he exerted in the secular realm.

Insight and events led Luther to attempt the reform of the church. Since the church, as an institution, was coextensive with the Western world he changed Europe. The reformation exploded out of theological theory into social practice where events called forth various responses.

In his 1520 "Open Letter to the Christian Nobility of the German Nation Concerning the Reform of the Christian Estate" he called for measures which could only be effected by revolution.[13] He instigated a movement which would deplace from power the rulers of the church and institute a substantially altered pattern of control and economic redistribution. He undertook this from without the bounds of the norms and laws which controlled his society. He dared to make his view of humanity's place in God's universe the fulcrum by which the lever of the pent-up frustrations of German society could be released for social and religious revolution.

Identifying himself as a fool by his culture's standards, he rested his foolishness on God's authority and set out to make his foolishness into the new norms of society. He attacked the legitimacy of his Roman opponents by asserting that they: were subject to temporal authority, did not possess the sole authority to interpret scripture, and were subject to decision by council. The abuses of Christendom to be reformed once authority was rightly determined reordered church, state, economy and academic life. In Luther's own writing it is clear that he understood that the reform of the spiritual life demanded fundamental changes in Christendom as a political-economic entity.

The other two treatises of 1520, "The Babylonian Captivity of the Church" and "The Freedom of a Christian," indicate Luther's complete break with Rome. They are revolutionary in consequence for the individual Christian's place in the scheme of meaning is changed. Though the spirit of the treatise on "Freedom" was conciliatory, its substance was evangelical and implied the consequences of the polemical "Babylonian Captivity."

Luther did not anticipate the consequences of his new appropriation of Christian faith and each stage of the drama probably surprised him as it opened. We will find it hard, however, to locate revolutions which developed as their instigators suspected they would. Revolutions, if they are understood as forces transforming the lives of men in fundamental ways and affecting the direction of human evolution, are too full of the ironies of history and providence for actors within them to comprehend. If Luther in 1517 had very little expectation of establishing the consequences of his theses in practice and no notion that the fierce opposition to his views which would tear Europe asunder, by 1520 he knew of the explosion of his world and had a faint hope that some of his beliefs articulated in the theses would bear fruit. Though he laughed at himself as perhaps only a court jester, his self-consciousness in 1520 would today be regarded as the mind of a revolutionary.

Luther's sense of the urgency of reform was deeply spiritual and bio-graphical. The thoroughgoingness of the spiritual reforms shook the entire temporal order of which they were a part. He tore away the old securities of life by breaking the back of Roman scholasticism and sacramentalism. He inspired the tearing up of the Empire by defying the Emperor. He encouraged the destruction in Germany of the power and property of the most important institution in the country. He provided the beginnings of a new university system. He provided a new conception of vocation which set man in a different place in the economy of the world. His contribution to development of the German literary language was immense and he provided the German Protestants with their catechisms and many of the hymns which warmed their lives. All of the above and much more he did while officially an outlaw whose sources of authority were themselves questioned by the prevailing models of authority. The model which was heretical and despised, articulated by an outlaw, became the new orthodoxy through blood and fire.

Scholarship on Luther, of course, has been strongly divided on the social influence of his teaching. The capture of Lutheranism by reactionary forces has made it difficult for scholars[14] to see the revolutionary social consequences of what began as a spiritual revolution and became a German revo-lution.

In his 1523 treatise on "Secular Authority" he expounded his theory of the two governments, one spiritual and the other secular. The two kingdoms are to be distinguished and permitted to coexist. God rules through both, but the secular rule is through governmental coercion and force, while the spiritual rule is through the Holy Spirit and love. The Christian ruled by love does not need the secular kingdom's rule but he honors it for its useful-ness to the whole world and recognizes that it has its authority from God.

In the treatise Luther's fear of social anarchy which was a constant threat
to sixteenth-century Germany inclines his hermeneutic toward reinforcing the
power of secular authority. He remains clear, however, that it is incompetent
and even asserts: "For God Almighty has made our rulers mad."[15]

His need for the protection of some authority against other authority,
his fear of anarchy, his expectation that the end of history was near, his
sense of God's providence all influenced his reading of scripture to the end
of discouraging the armed overthrow of authority. However, because the spiritual realm is not separate from the temporal realm, the forces unleashed in
the spiritual realm upset the temporal realm. The distinction between the
spiritual and the secular kingdom gives an impression of a doctrine of dis-
interest in the secular kingdom. It is true that Luther knew more about the
spiritual realm than he did about sociology. But in his hands the doctrine
became a weapon for change. He repeatedly accused the Pope of being too
worldly and he demanded that the temporal realm use its power to reform the
administration of the spiritual realm. On the other hand he could use the
distinction to strengthen secular government from Papal interference. The
doctrine served both to enable him to attack the political privileges of
Rome while guaranteeing the protection of orderly German government from left-
wing Christian aspects of the movement he had started.

His polemics against the peasants who rose against the social order in
1525 have seemed to separate Luther from the ranks of the world's revolutionaries. It is true he had warned the rulers to meet the peasants' grievances,
it is also true that if Germany were to have any stability it could not
tolerate destructive armies of rebels within its order. However, Luther will
always be justly criticized for failing to recognize the voice of God in the
legitimate grievances of the peasants. The peasants were the poor of the

world and they deserved a predisposition from the ministers of God for the hearing of their case. The principle of the two kingdoms in Luther's hands demanded passive suffering from the peasants and bloody repression from the princes. Such an outcome of the principle itself invalidates the principle. There can be no justification of Luther's encouragement of the princes in their bloody suppression.

To indicate that Luther failed the poor and consequently failed God in the matter regarding the peasants' rebellion does not mean he was not a revolutionary. By 1525 his movement was far enough advanced to expect some success, the peasants threatened to undo the revolution. He protected his revolution by beating off the idealists and the poor to the left of the movement. Such is the irony turned into tragedy of revolution.

Calvinist Revolutionaries

Conservative Methodist historians quote the cliche with approval that it was John Wesley's evangelical movement which saved England from revolution. The same historians seem to ignore (1) that, though the French revolution of the eighteenth century was troublesome, perhaps England could have used its own revolution then. But more importantly they forget (2) that England had already had its revolution, and it had been a Calvinist one in the 1640's.

The English Calvinists (1560-1690) were a new social-religious type. They were radically different in their theology and politics from the medieval synthesis, the Renaissance politicians as seen in Machiavelli, or the early reformers. They were makers of revolution, the disciplined saints who bashed England through a period of transition and had only an insignificant place to play after the Restoration and the revival of Lockean politics. (1) Their execution (or murder) of King Charles I was a thorough inquiry into the meaning of monarchy itself. It was judicial and thoughtful. (2) Their armies,

with discipline, representative councils and mass political education, were
distinctively their own. (3) They literally set out to make and then remake
the structure of their country through the writing of a constitution.
(4) Demands for reform of the whole system were constantly made public.
(5) New groups of voluntary association and ideological commitment were
formed to implement the reforms. (6) Political journalism appeared to serve
the needs of this newly created reforming public.[16]

These parties of revolutionary colonists assumed responsibility for a
world which God controlled and in which he demanded that his saints engage in
continuous disciplined war against the allies of Satan. They approached
politics not for their own interests nor with any trust in the system; they
approached it as intra-worldly ascetics who had a struggle on their hands
and in the struggle was found religious joy and a security to match the
terrors of the old age that was passing.

The Calvinists brought their reforming faith against the compromises
of the Elizabethan settlement, and they discovered that in the process of
elaborating their theology with its radical emphasis upon the sovereignty of
God and the fall of humanity, the old political models were destroyed. The
Puritan preachers with their literature on the soul's quest for salvation,
the bitter struggle with the devil, the covenant voluntarily established with
God, had prefigured the revolution. Salvation could be won alone, but it was
better to win it in company, and all of England seemed like a goodly company
in the seventeenth century.

Feudal politics was conducted under the banner of the great chain of
being. All of the world, humanity, nature and spirit, were the overflowing of
being itself and were properly arranged in hierarchies of order. The human
hierarchies held, even when seemingly absurd, with great tenacity because

they were part of the total chain which had proper places for archbishops, bishops, clerics, etc. There was really no room for the fall and rebellion within the system. The great chain of being of course restricted the freedom of any God who would be sovereign, or the influence of any Satan creating chaos, and made revolt on the part of humanity hard to comprehend. Calvinism's God was too free for the chain of being model to hold, and the effects of human fall were too catastrophic for the nice orders of the chain, so people were freed into a more warlike and chaotic world where hierarchies were continually subject to challenge. One could say the despotism of Calvin's God relativized the hierarchies of the chain of being. Similarly the replacement of the organic models of the state freed men to get about remaking the state. To the Calvinists the model of the state as an organic body did not explain the tensions within it. Rather than an indissoluble body with a known head, the state was a ship and the captain of the ship of state could be deplaced by mutiny if his actions obviously threatened the safety of others on board. Not mystery in describing the state but relationships of command and discipline were preferred by the Calvinists.

The group of exiles from England known as the Marian exiles (1553-1558) typify this Calvinist revolutionary spirit. This group of about eight hundred Protestants was composed of roughly one-half ministers and theological students, one-third gentlemen, and others. The predominance of the clerical intellectuals in the group gave it influence out of proportion to its size as it disbanded to various cities in southern Germany and Switzerland. For five years these Englishmen lived as exiles outside of jurisdiction as free people. The intellectuals spent their time fighting over church constitutions and formulating an ideology which could give them a place in the time of transition. Alienated and outlawed, they developed a justification

for revolution in a series of writings addressed to their countrymen. John
Knox defined his office in terms of the office of prophet and from this
position argued that "the prophet of God sometimes may teach treason against
kings." Their pamphlets became the traces of rebellion.

Satan was seen to be ruling the institutions of humanity and the de-
nunciations of the Geneva-based Englishmen described the world in nearly
Manichean terms. The prophet was set against the state in the "spirit of
righteous judgment." Knox and Goodman moved beyond the French Protestants'
justification of resistance to the justification of revolution. "Later in
his life, when Knox was asked whether godly subjects might overthrow an ungodly
prince, he answered briefly, raising no legal or moral problems: 'If they are
able.'"[17] Knox moved from gradualism through reformism, resistance to revolution, and in many ways the die for revolution in England in the seventeenth
century was cast when these Marian exiles returned to England in the mid-
sixteenth century.

The exiles and the parties which grew out of their influence and
those troubled times were "strangers" who thought of themselves as saints
seeking a new order; they were distinguished from their compatriots by self-
assurance, daring and discipline. The band of saints confronts the world as
in war; they watch and calculate their chances. Their patterns of organization reflect both the new order they long for and the necessary pragmatic
compromises. The living of their sainthood produces a new kind of politics.
They destroy the old order and the destruction is thoroughgoing because they
have a vision of the new world.[18] Within themselves their faith provides a
healing for the chaos of the times which permits them to function politically.
Once the revolution has spent its force, the ideological equipment which made
them revolutionaries puts them ill at ease and they feel alienated once again:

What a misfit I've become
. . . I feel a foreigner in my land.[19]

Christian faith urges human liberation. Resistance to liberation and to the growing forces of liberation produces the convulsion of revolution. The figures and movements we have examined in Christian revolutions have not been primarily concerned to avoid violence nor have they been awed by the previous settlements which were interfering with the freedom of the Christian people.

The circumstances in all the revolutions examined were different, and the meaning of liberty itself changed in the different epochs. The theological students supporting Gregory, Luther and Knox were certainly engaged in different causes, but all were in a sense appropriate to their time, expanding the possibilities of freedom, reforming the church, and demanding a new political order. The Christian revolutionaries were all transitional figures caught between systems, and they were articulating a new model of heaven and earth in which they hoped they could find meaning. All were by the prevailing standards of their times either exiles, outlaws or both, and yet all were certain that by the power which was ultimate their actions were appropriate.

The Christian revolutionaries discussed here would all have appeared fanatical to some of their contemporaries and self-righteous to many more. Such characteristics are probably the burden of those who initiate new epochs. In no cases were the final settlements left in the hands of the revolutionaries discussed. Often the final world was left in antithetical or at least compromising hands, but when it is all discussed and over-analyzed it was probably more interesting to have the first word rather than the last.[20]

The revolutionary potential of the Christian faith has been unleashed many times, though the above discussion only points to the potential in Jesus' actions and its unfolding in three quite different cases. Though Rosemary

Ruether's discussion of three schemes of salvation present in Christian faith
(apocalypse, inward journey and grand master plan) is quite helpful, she
underestimates the explosive power in the faith. She argues:

> Potentially, the elements of the Christian worldview could
> be formulated in a social revolutionary manner, but, in
> actuality, this did not occur and could not occur until
> Christendom itself--that society founded on the idea of
> the church as the final age of world history--went into
> dissolution.[21]

Certainly this is not the case, unless we deny Gregory, Luther and the English
Calvinists the title. And in that case it would be hard to identify anyone
as revolutionaries. If it is correct that Christian faith and social crisis
have repeatedly produced revolutionary change, then it may follow that
reliance on anti-Christian sources for understanding revolution may not be
obligatory. The view argued for so far is appreciative but critical of both
Moltmann and Ruether. Moltmann over-emphasizes the early church's contribution to revolutionary change, while Ruether neglects to see revolutionary
change in Christian movements which transformed their times.

The proclamation by Jesus of the Kingdom of God gave a subversive
cast to his teaching and contributed to his political death and to the
eternal relevance of his message. Gregory VII confused the Kingdom of God
with the church, but contributed significantly in furthering the freedom of
the church and the political dualism of the West. Luther disconnected the
Kingdom of God from both the church and the secular government and altered
forever the evolution of those institutions. The Puritans perceived the
essential revolutionary thrust of the Kingdom and in their struggle laid the
groundwork for parliamentary government and a wide range of political free-
doms.

The churches played a significant role in preparing for the American war of independence, but in the French revolution, which became the model for revolutionary writing, the church was largely in the forces of counter revolution. In nineteenth century Europe the church was in alliance with capitalism and status quo politics to a degree which disassociated it from the revolutionary movements.

In the person of Karl Marx, revolutionary thought found its architect for the modern age. An exiled German Doctor of Philosophy, he was to wrap his philosophy of revolution in a fundamentally anti-Christian position. His critique of religion is so profound and his theory of revolution so influential, that all interested in the deeper aspects of social change must take account of him.

IV. THE REVOLUTIONARY ANTI-KINGDOM OF KARL MARX

Karl Marx is rightly appreciated today as a revolutionary humanist. Long after his particularized observations about the nineteenth century have faded in importance, his vision of a new world in which humanity is liberated continues to inspire action. In a world in which vision is required, Robert C. Tucker has found the utopian elements of Marx's thoughts to be his most important contribution. Confronting the dilemmas of the twentieth century, Tucker finds Marx's hope relevant, "in an age when utopianism has become the only realism."[1]

Engels buried his friend Karl Marx with the claim that he was "before all else a revolutionist." The revolution that Marx prepared the way for was more than the street fighting and the lost urban revolts he supported during his life. His thought, encompassing all of human history, was an attempt to unravel the secrets of society and prepare it for its transformation. His plans for change in institutions were not deterred by an unchangeable nature of humanity, for he thought that human nature itself would be changed.

Marx provides a philosophy of history which is fundamentally that of the class struggle. The struggle will increase in ferocity, and it will build to its climax. The climax of this history, the revolution, will produce a new stage of history in which the previous contradictions among the classes will be overcome. Human nature, which includes the capacity for remaking that nature, will be remade in this new history which is, in a sense, the only history for Marx because everything preceding the revolution was prehistory. This model of history is fundamental in that it controls all other conclusions. Marx cannot be a reformer in morals, religion, economics or politics because

48

he is a revolutionist. His model is not of evolution, though he admired Darwin. His model is of a break with the past, with an overcoming of the past.

For Marx the politics of Hegel could not be tolerated, for it was too realistic. It allowed for the compromise of the ideal with the real, and finally it promised only spiritual liberation. Marx demanded absolute bodily liberation, and that was not possible in the real politics of Germany or in Hegel's philosophy of politics. Only in a new day could Marx's ideal be realized, and that required revolution. Finally, for Marx, no politics could be tolerated, and his essential romantic anarchism stands exposed in his concept of the withering away of the state. The withering of the state again presupposed revolution, the ending of this exploitative chapter of history.

Hegel longed for freedom within the state. Marx knew that the state was antithetical to freedom. Even a socialist state would suppress freedom. Ultimately his thirst for the free development of mankind rested not upon socialism but upon anarchism, the removal of humanity's domination of humanity. In the acknowledgment of the utopian character of Marx's thinking is contained the recognition of his vision of society without government. His vision of the classless society then is an anti-kingdom view. He utilizes elements of the classical religious protest against the existing governments and his eschatology is governmentless.

His position to the student of religious movements is that of an apocalyptic prophet. He expects mankind to be saved from the evils that plague them. The salvation can only come at the end of an epoch of history, and then it can only come through destruction. The proletariat for Marx bear the role of the chosen people. To be saved one must become part of this one class, which will be the universal class in the classless epoch after the revolution. As a proclaimer of the apocalypse, he used the language of his day to express his message and to examine the signs of the times. He was intolerant of other claimants to the interpretation of the apocalypse, as apocalyptic thinkers often are. Particularly, he was critical of the utopian socialists who were so close to him in thinking but who did not realize that the transformation could only come through bloody struggle.

His philosophy of history helped him to see many things. Because he believed that the struggle was going to become more severe, he was free to see clearly the depths of exploitation and dehumanization that characterized developing capitalism. However, he may also have been shielded by his vision from seeing possible developments within capitalism which would ally the workers with the capitalists. He was free to view politics as characterized by brutality and corruption, but he may have been prevented from seeing the bonds of trust and mutuality which kept the system going because he trusted in its demise.

Marx is not the first with a religious vision to reject violently the religious assumptions of others. He is perhaps the most important of those who, in the nineteenth century, contributed to supplanting traditional religious language from positions of influence by substituting scientific language replete with religious assumptions. His attack upon traditional religion and morality lies close to the heart of his thinking. Before examining his critique of religion it is worth noting how he compared his philosophy of history to the early Christian hope in the eschaton.

> The dream of the imminent destruction of the world inspired the
> early Christians in their struggle with the Roman world empire
> and gave them a certainty of victory. Scientific insight into
> the unavoidable and continuing disintegration of the dominant
> order of society, constantly visible before our eyes, and the
> increasingly passionate whipping of the masses by the old
> government specters, as well as the gigantically advancing

positive development of the means of production--all this
serves as a guarantee that at the moment of outbreak of a
real proletarian revolution its very conditions (even if
surely not idyllic ones) will directly bring forth the next
modus operandi.[2]

Karl Marx and the End of Religion

Today, several considerations demand a serious rethinking of Marx's

analysis of religion. For too long Marx's attack on religion has obscured

the profundity of his investigations into the relationship of religion and

the ills of society. The counterattacks of religious people have prevented a

full appreciation of the truth in Marx's critique. The West, no longer

severely threatened by Communism, can now freely investigate Marx's critique

of religion and society and, in the confidence of its new maturity, Marxism

can tolerate a new openness to rethinking Marx's position on religion. The

issue of Marx's adequacy and accuracy is also raised by Christian polemicists

announcing the end of religion in the West. The optimism of the revolution-

ary theologians is closer to the thought of the optimism of Karl Marx, the

prophet of the revolutionary apocalypse; whereas his doctrine of alienation

has more in common with the realistic critics of the new theologians. The

dialogue between Christian theologians and Marxist philosophers has reached

the point where it can profitably focus on the basic tenets of their respec-

tive ideologies. Such a focus must consider divisive issues such as the

nature of religion as well as areas of mutual agreement.

Marx said a great deal about religion, and many of his points cannot

easily be synthesized. Often he only repeated what Comte, Saint-Simon, Hegel,

Feuerbach and others had said. Religion was understood by Marx to consist of

a body of concepts. His understanding of religion as a system of doctrine or

collection of ideas to interpret the world was a product of nineteenth-century

German scholarship. Marx analyzed religion as an ideology brilliantly, but he knew little of religion as the cumulative tradition and ritual of a culture, and even less of religion as a deeply personal encounter with that which is regarded as ultimate or transcendent. Though his treatment of religion as essentially ideology reflected the level of scholarship of his time, Marx's connection of this ideology with humanity's alienation was a suggestive and original contribution. Later Marxist scholarship has neglected this insight in Marx while exaggerating the importance of what he said about religion as class ideology.

In Marx's view, religion was an inverted world-consciousness which would disappear when the world was set right. Humanity would not need its opium in the new world which the logic of history and the Marxists would bring to realization. Religion was not fundamental to human nature, but was rather a by-product of his estrangement, which in turn was due to the system of production. It is the connection of religion with estrangement or alienation that provides Marx with a tool of analysis which cuts very deeply into the many-layered compound of religion. This conception of alienation provided his later social criticism with its driving moral power. Consideration of Marx's critique of religion, then, provides a suggestive and provocative hypothesis for the study of religion as well as revealing the origins of the Marxist critique of society.

Marx regarded the rational critique of religion as unlikely to have much effect on religious belief, but he did expect that the direct assault upon human alienation, when successful, would lead to religion's death as a by-product. If religion is dependent upon alienation, the elimination of alienation would be accompanied by the disappearance of religion. Marx's understanding, critique, and triumph over religion were all related to his

concept of alienation. Therefore, the first prerequisite for an understanding of Marx on religion is a comprehension of this concept.

Alienation and Religion in Hegel and Feuerbach

The root idea of alienation is borrowed from Hegel, but Marx elabor-
ates it and develops it in ways foreign to Hegel. Hegel drew the concept
from Christianity's doctrine of the fall, which held that humanity's estrangement from one another and the source of creation was cosmic in scope and pre-
historic in origin. Hegel demythologized and rationalized the stories of the
fall and connected them with the creation. The content of a fallen nature
and a fallen humanity seemed appropriate to Hegel, but the form in which they
had been stated was awkward. Hegel translated the concept of alienation from
theology to the language of social philosophy. The following discussion of
Hegel's use of alienation examines his doctrine of human nature, much of
which Marx retained long after he had rejected Hegelian metaphysics. Self-
estrangement (Selbst-Entfremdung) describes humanity's fallen state. In this
state people are neither at peace with themselves nor with their fellows.
Humanity creates law, but cannot obey it. A person makes resolutions, but
conflicts develop within oneself. One finds oneself rejecting the society
which depends upon participation. The society comes to be viewed as an alien
force which frustrates the individual. Hegel calls this treatment of society
as an alien force Vergegenstandlichung, meaning that one no longer recognizes
products as one's own but regards them as an alien force.[3] The subject no
longer recognizes the object as part of oneself. Hegel's use of alienation
points to a fundamental antithesis between what humanity is and what it ought
to be. This contrast between existence and essence in anthropology is quite
Pauline in character, but Hegel's thought possesses an optimism foreign to

the theologians who have followed Paul closely. This optimism, expressed in terms of the ideal replacing the real, is due partially to a neglect of actual historical observation (e.g., his illusions about the Prussian state), but also to his belief in the ultimate dependence of the real upon the rational. In his system reconciliation of the ideal and the real was expected as the mind overcame the barrier between humanity and society. By increasing self-knowledge and technical knowledge, one could come to understand and master the world and come to one's own Aneignung. As one develops power, one can expect progress and eventually feel at home in the world.

For Hegel, of course, humanity's reconciliation with the world is part of the Absolute's reconciliation with the world which is external from it, but Marx takes over the concept of alienation only as it relates to social phenomena. Hegel's vision of humanity incorporated religious themes, but it gave to religion itself only the temporary role of bearing truth in symbolic form until philosophy could disentangle the truth from symbolism. Though Hegel never himself abandoned religion and many of his passages can be taken to mean that the Christian religion and Hegelian philosophy say the same thing only in different forms, it seems a safe minimal statement that Hegel expected "rational" humanity to use philosophy rather than theology to understand reality.

In addition to saying that religious beliefs expressed, if only symbolically, the essence of reality, Hegel taught that religion expresses the anxieties of estranged humanity. The otherworldliness of religion is due fundamentally to unhappiness in this world, according to Hegel. Marx was to expand upon this theme, but Marx's critique of religion was also dependent upon Feuerbach, and an examination of his thought on alienation and religion must precede an exposition of Marx's answer to the problem.

Feuerbach moved from Hegelianism through Left Hegelianism to materialistic humanism. He saw himself displacing the abstract reason of Hegel by
reference to the concrete thinking of people. He summarized his own move from
Hegel to humanism thus, "God was my first thought; reason, my second; and man,
my third and last." Mind lacks the autonomy it had in Hegel; rather, all
thought is derivative from actual thinking persons. Thought is regarded as a
social product which originates only as people begin to have social intercourse with each other. Thought is the attempt to communicate the world,
encountered only in experience, to other people. Proper thought, for
Feuerbach, depends upon the recognition of its social function and its derivative character.

Some critics have regarded Feuerbach as a materialist, others as a
humanist. The combination of the two labels avoids certain misunderstandings
which arise if either is used alone. Humanity is supreme in Feuerbach's
thought, but not independent of his material base. "Man is what he eats."
Humanity's social life, morals, and intellectual life are all dependent on
his physical well-being. The race is the product of its cultural history,
but it never escapes the material basis of its existence.

Feuerbach believes that the essence of humanity is found in his social
relationships. Humanity in community is the proper object of knowledge. Art,
religion, philosophy, and science are regarded as expressions of humanity's
social intercourse. Religious illusions are based upon the failure to recognize humanity's essence in community. Thinkers have objectified and projected
humanity to the neglect of living people. The images of religion reflect this
distorted projection of humanity and have no material content. Feuerbach holds,
though, that the heart of the gospel is correct even if confusedly expressed.
"God is love" properly means that people fulfill themselves in human

relationships. The theological language hides the truth it was intended to express.

Feuerbach's The Essence of Christianity is in many places a tedious, pretentious work. It is unhistorical, and references do not always support the conclusion Feuerbach intended they should. It reflects the mid-nineteenth century romanticism which seems so foreign today. But his work is reflected in our current debates and undergirds the discourse which uses the language of "I and Thou" and "alienation" or "estrangement."

Barth has seen in Feuerbach the reductio ad absurdum of all theologies which place their trust in anthropological analysis. For Barth the issue between Feuerbach's atheism and Christian theology narrows down to whether or not Feuerbach's optimism about humanity was valid. Barth can dismiss Feuerbach because the latter, so completely a man of his time, never faced the meaning of evil and death. No one, claims Barth, who honestly faced evil and death could fall under "the most illusory of all illusions to suppose that the essence of God is the essence of man."[4]

Marxists have given Marx credit for discovering the economic and social origins of religious illusions, but Feuerbach laid the foundations upon which Marx built. Feuerbach wrote, for example:

> The impoverishing of the real world and the enriching of God is one act. Only the poor man has a rich God. God springs out of the feeling of a want; what man is in need of, whether this be a definite and therefore conscious, or an unconscious need--that is God.[5]

> The idea of the species becomes the idea of God, who again is himself an individual being, but is distinguished from human individuals in this, that he possesses their qualities according to the measure of the species.[6]

Feuerbach remains a Left Hegelian in regarding thinking as the way to overcome estrangement. Thought is the most truly human activity. Though he argues, "Politics must become our religion," he is thinking of discussion

about political principles and not actual political participation in the
material concerns of society.

Marx used Feuerbach as a reservoir of concepts which he could draw
upon and utilize in his own distinctive way. The critique of Ludwig Feuerbach
in the eleven famous theses has obscured Marx's dependence on Feuerbach.
Marx tended to criticize most thoroughly those who held positions similar to
his own. But in his National Economy and Philosophy he said, "There is no
way to truth and freedom save through Feuerbach--the bath of fire which is
the purgatory through which the present age must pass."[7]

Marx obtained from Feuerbach the idea that all the expressions of
human creativity have their basis in material needs. Therefore, according
to Marx, humanity's material needs and not ideas were primary. The primacy
of humanity's material needs was the perspective which Marx used to criticize
Hegel's idealism. Rather than turning Hegel's system upside down, as he
claimed, he put it in dead storage and utilized it as a source of ideas from
which he could draw eclectically. He endorsed Feuerbach's attack upon religion, carrying it even further. Likewise he fastened upon humanity realizing
its essence in social relationships as a key to explaining the gap between
the Hegelian ideal and the empirical reality of social relationships. But
Marx attacked the idea of "essences" as overly abstract and plunged beneath
social relationships to production relationships as the key to understanding
humanity. When Marx declares, "It is not consciousness that determines being,
but it is social being that determines consciousness,"[8] meaning the activity
of human production, he is reflecting his debt to Feuerbach and his opposition
to Hegel.

Marx's break with Feuerbach is represented in the Eleven Theses written
in 1845 but not published until Engels included them as an appendix to his own

Ludwig Feuerbach in 1888. The major criticism Marx levels at Feuerbach is
that he undervalues the significance of practical or revolutionary activity.
This charge is raised in several forms in the eleven points and can be regarded as the thesis of the Theses. Marx regards as sound the Feuerbachian dis-
missal of religion as illusion, but it does not pursue the analysis far enough
to suit Marx. The need, according to Marx, was for an explanation of religion
in terms of the estrangement humanity felt due to the system of production
which it had created. The tendency for people to project the secular onto an
imaginary heaven can be explained by the "self-cleavage and self-contradictoriness of this secular basis."[9] Once the self-contradictoriness of contemporary society is seen as the basis of illusion, the task is to change the
society. While it is helpful to realize that Feuerbach's concept of alienation is more psychological and Marx's sociological, Marx exaggerated Feuerbach's individualism. Feuerbach would not have denied that religion was a
social product; every human creation reflected humanity in community, but he
most likely would have replied to Marx that, historically, religion is an
individual product as well as a social product.

Alienation

It is difficult to build a systematic account of Marx's concept of
alienation.[10] There are passages in his writings on alienation which are not
considered in this chapter, which presupposes his Hegelian-Feuerbachian background to illumine points on which Marx himself is unclear.

Alienation for Marx occurs when the product of human labor is set up
to frustrate the drive for self-affirmation. Humanity's need for self-
affirmation prompts one to make products which reflect oneself and meet other
needs. By possessing products one expands oneself and still possesses oneself.
One needs work to realize self-identity by enjoying work which contains the

self. But the enjoyment of one's produce may be frustrated if the product
is set up against the producer. This has happened. Humanity's self-creations
have become objectified and turned against the producer, resulting in frustration.

> The alienation of the worker in his product means not only
> that his labour becomes an object, takes on its own exist-
> ence, but that it exists outside him independently, and
> alien to him, and that it stands opposed to him as an
> autonomous power. The life which he has given to the object
> sets itself against him as an alien and hostile force.[11]

The broader context of the above definition of alienation implies that Marx
is thinking of production in a capitalist economy. Alienation is minimized
in primitive communities in which, for the most part, one produces to satisfy
one's own wants; but increased production and particularly the division of
labor decrease a person's involvement with products. Alienation arises from
the system of production; the system of production is dependent upon the
division of labor, private property and money. The division of labor seems
to be the fundamental factor: money, beginning as a means of exchange to make
the division of labor function more smoothly, rises to a position of the
"visible deity" and "universal whore." Private property seems to be an effect
rather than a basic cause of alienation.[12] It is the original division of
labor which separated humanity from its product and which prepared the way for
modern capitalism and all of its dehumanizing effects. In a money economy in
which the worker sells labor, labor loses any satisfaction value and only
serves to obtain money. The worker in a sense is selling himself, and for a
low price. The advantageous position of the capitalist allows him to purchase
the labor cheaply and to utilize the surplus value to increase the gap between
the capitalist and the proletarian. The proletarian cannot find work self-
affirming, and a fundamental human drive is unmet. Other frustrations result

from this basic failure to fulfill oneself in one's work; many of these frustrations are described by Marx as alienation.

Though Marx only rarely distinguishes carefully between his various uses of alienation, there seem to be six uses which can be distinguished. (1) The producer finds work unsatisfying because the division of labor assures that the worker does only one job which, in the modern industrial world, progressively takes on the character of serving a machine. The laborer's work is not a satisfying end but only a means to obtain money to satisfy wants. The laborer's human potentialities are not developed, and the producer finds work boring. This basic dissatisfaction with one's work is a central meaning of the alienation of labor for Marx. (2) Alienation is used to mean that the worker's product is turned against oneself. The capitalist buys the worker's labor and uses the products to the detriment of the worker. The capitalist uses his profit which is really surplus labor to buy more labor-saving machines and thereby reduces the value of the labor which the proletariat has to sell. The product, an extension of the worker's psyche, is not only foreign to him but turned against him. (3) Alienation is used to refer to the fact that labor is treated as a commodity. Human values are lost sight of in capitalist society, where one's labor is purchasable in the same way as a pair of shoes. (4) Alienation refers to the worker's poverty in the midst of plenty. The production system is geared to keep labor cheap, and the value of labor will decline as the advantages of the capitalist increase. (5) Psychological alienation depends upon the above forms of alienation and is very similar to dissatisfaction with one's work. It has been distinguished here from the first kind of alienation because it represents the extension of that dissatisfaction to the totality of man's life. The hours spent at work are fundamental, and if they are not satisfying, all of life is tainted. If one cannot

fulfill the need for self-affirmation at work then the whole personality is
distorted. (6) In addition to a universal psychological alienation,
humanity's social products are distorted. The creations of the state,
bourgeois morality, and religion are all compensations and/or adjustments to
alienated humanity. These social products, or at least the theory about these
institutions, can be referred to as ideological alienation.

Marx on Religion

Religion to Marx was the fantastic reflection in people's minds of
the oppressive forces of the productive world. Religion belonged to the
world of illusion; he called it a "reverse world-consciousness." The otherworldliness of religion was a projection of humanity's unrealized hopes for
this world. It was true that humanity proposed plans and that an alien force
controlled humanity's destiny, but it was the capitalist mode of production,
not a supernatural God, which was the alien controlling force. Marx, in other
words, accepts the deus ex machina theology but defines deus as the capitalist
mode of production.

Religion reveals two things: human distress and protest against distress. But religion betrays humanity by failing to grapple with the source
of distress and by furnishing nothing more than comforting illusions. As one
is diminished when his product is alienated, so humanity is diminished when
it projects its desires and hopes onto an alien supernatural being. The projection of human desires and hopes into another world comforts humanity in
its sorrow but prevents it from dealing realistically with the source of his
anguish.

The fundamental basis of all religious criticism is, for Marx, "Man
makes religion, religion does not make man."[13] This succinct thesis asserts

that religion is a human product completely understandable in terms of psychological, sociological and especially economic analysis. As well as rejecting
the transcendent element in religion, the thesis asserts that religion does
not fulfill human aspirations. For Marx, religion fails to fulfill its claims
both metaphysically and ethically.

Marx's conclusion that religion would disappear with the overcoming
of alienation is consistent with his total analysis of religion. But there
were other factors which drove Marx to posit the end of religion. His philosophical materialism, scientism, hatred of the status quo, and militant
atheism all encouraged him to regard religion as a contingent phenomenon.

Social criticism and the investigation of religion were inextricably
linked. Religion was a social product; it was the ideological product of
people whose social lives were corrupted by a system of production which
alienated them from their product and from one another. The conclusion that
productive systems caused people to create ideologies to hide the truth about
their alienation provided Marx with an analytical device to separate truth
from illusion in religion. Theology, according to Marx, presented truths
about human nature but only in an unrecognizable way. Religion revealed the
distortions of life. Therefore the critique of religion could, after the
gods were dismissed as illusory, lead to an understanding of human alienation
in society. If properly undertaken, the analysis of religion led to an
analysis of its sources, the system of production, and to attempts to change
the alienating system of production. Marx's statement of the relationship
of social criticism to the criticism of religion reveals the inseparability
of the two critiques:

> For Germany the criticism of religion is in the main complete,
> and criticism of religion is the premise of all criticism. . . .
> The immediate task of philosophy, which is at the service of

history once the saintly form of human self-alienation
has been unmasked, is to unmask self-alienation in its
unholy forms. Thus the criticism of heaven turns into
the criticism of the earth, the criticism of religion
into the criticism of right and the criticism of
theology into the criticism of politics.[14]

Marx's claim that social criticism depended upon the criticism of

religion was more than a methodological move. The assertion reflected his

own intellectual development. His early attack upon theological Hegelianism

resulted in his losing the opportunity to lecture in philosophy. His early

writings focus on the connections he saw between his study of religion and

his conclusions about the nature of mankind. In his later writings, particu-

larly in Das Kapital, the symptoms of alienation are translated into the

symptoms of the division of labor. The sociology of religion origins of

Marxist science are evident when due account is given to the fact that in the

earlier writing the division of labor was the cause of alienation. The cor-

respondence between the elderly Marx and Engels reveals the continuing passion

to analyze religion and the continuing hope for its demise. Though Marx must

be regarded as an enemy of religion, he was an enemy who saw clearly the deep

roots religion had in the human soul.

Religion which served to allay fears and to promote hope and also

served to promote or weaken a certain social system was, by Marx's definition,

ideology. If religion served to strengthen a certain social situation which

gave advantage to a particular class, that religion could be treated as class

ideology. Religious movements could best be explained, Marx thought, by the

sociological functions of the religion and the given class structure. Hence

the religious history of the East was explained by the lack of private

property and Protestantism by the bourgeois character of Europe. Certainly

an argument that religion often (probably usually) sanctioned the given

social structures could be made, and in this sense it would be a class
ideology according to Marx's definitions. But there are cases where religion
has undercut accepted social patterns and, more importantly, where the same
classes have different religions or where radically different religious views
are compatible with various political ideologies. The idea of religion as a
class ideology has been developed by later Marxists, but as an analytical
device it is far less valuable than the insight that religion results from
alienation. The whole discussion of the relationship of class interests and
economic position to religious views has been more fruitfully developed by
Max Weber, who tried to refute Marxian economic determinism. But the conclusion to the debate over the Weber-Tawney thesis is far from settled.
Other interests than class position have usually been in the forefront of the
minds of religious innovators, and any attempt to reduce religion to class
ideology is doomed to frustration. Some attention must be directed to the
claims and institutions of religion itself, rather than focusing all attention
on its social spin-off.

Marx's essay on the Jewish question illustrates very clearly his analysis of religion and hopes of eliminating it. Marx criticizes Bauer's recom-
mendation that the only solution to the Jewish problem was for the Jews to
surrender their faith. The problem of the alienation of the Jew is too deep
to be solved either by the abandonment of their faith (his father had tried
that route to freedom) or by receiving complete toleration by the Christian
state. The alienation of the Jew whose essence was reflected, for Marx, in
the bourgeois character of the modern world could not be eliminated apart
from the emancipation of humanity. For Marx, the unreality of the Jewish
religious essence was merely an idealized reflection of his practical, i.e.,
economic, needs. Marx protests too loudly in his denunciation of Judaism,

leading some authorities to conclude that much of the essence of nineteenth-century German Judaism remains in Marx's philosophy.[15] Marx's hatred of the bourgeoisie reinforced his antipathy toward Judaism because he regarded it as encouraging bourgeois values.

> As soon as society succeeds in abolishing the empirical essence of Judaism, the huckster, and the conditions which produce him, the Jew will become impossible because his consciousness will no longer have a corresponding object. . . .
> The social emancipation of the Jew is the emancipation of society from Judaism.[16]

Marx attempts to lift the Jewish question out of its theological context into its social-economic context and to argue that particular expressions of the fracturing of the human community should not be considered in isolation. The whole problem, the emancipation of humanity, was the only context large enough for the consideration of the emancipation of the Jews. But in Marx's larger context, the emancipation of the Jews became the destruction of all of Judaism's distinctive features.

Another theme of Marx's critique of religion was drawn from the conflict between science and religion. He regarded religion as illusion and expected science continually to narrow the field in which theology was considered competent to furnish answers. Dogmatic theology was seen as a substitute for scientific answers and as such was clearly open to attack. Marx had few illusions, though, that science would drive religion from people's minds; only the social revolution which would eliminate the root cause of alienation could do that. Marx's views on the science and religion conflict were neither more nor less profound than those of many other nineteenth-century religious skeptics. Greater humility on the part of both scientists and theologians has moved the debate beyond the Marxian analysis. In fact the debate seems to have quieted, with scientist and theologian marking off different spheres of discourse for their respective disciplines.

Critique of Marx on Religion

Marx's analysis of religion has advanced the study of religion. It can never again adequately be studied in isolation from the total cultural-social matrix in which it finds expression. More forcefully than his predecessors, he made the point that religion can be a bastion of social conservatism. He deepened the critique of religion by showing that the suffering of humanity accounted for and compensated for in various ways by religion, had social as well as individual origins. His writings are full of tantalizing suggestions and hypotheses for the further investigation of religion.

To recognize the value of Marx's thesis that religion springs from human alienation is not, however, to accept it as established. Several considerations count against the acceptance of the thesis as it was expressed by Marx.

1. It is crucial to Marx's argument that the system of production be, in some important sense, regarded as fundamental and other social institutions as derivative. The changes in the system of production through the ages, for Marx, are the keys which unlock the meaning of history.

The thesis that the system of production is fundamental has been interpreted as an expression of a rather simple materialism, asserting as Feuerbach did that man must eat before he can create. Humanity depends upon the satisfaction of material wants and normally strives to fulfill them before turning to ideological expression. This is true as far as it goes. There is nothing in this position, however, to justify regarding a religion in all of its expressions as determined by, for example, slash and burn agriculture or capitalism.

The thesis has also been taken to mean that the evolution of the system of production occurred prior to and was therefore in some way determinative of the evolution of other institutions. William H. McNeil has indirectly challenged the chronological priority of systems of production by arguing in The Rise of the West that the first important division of labor in the Tigris and Euphrates civilization was between priests and laity and that the surplus product which made possible further division of labor was first amassed by the priests as offerings to the gods. If McNeil is correct, religious belief preceded the first important division of labor, rather than being a by-product of the system of production.

There are many hazards in attempting to analyze any contemporary social structure by its postulated origins, and occasionally Marx revealed an awareness of these hazards. He once wrote in attack against those who romanticized Germany's past and explained German institutions on the basis of their Teutonic origins: "It is common knowledge that the forest echoes back what you shout into it. So peace to the ancient Teutonic forests!" Still, Marx's discussion of religion slips into the genetic fallacy, the supposition that the primitive origins of a social institution explain its contemporary relevance.

The meaning of his thesis which most interested Marx was the bold assertion that the character of all of humanity's ideological expressions was determined by the system of production. Education, philosophy, religion, etc., were to be regarded as dependent upon the economic system; changes in the economic system would cause corresponding changes in the ideological expressions of the economic system. Modern social science has moved away from positing one institution as fundamental and tends to regard all viable social institutions as serving important functions in one's social life and constantly interacting with one another. Characteristics of a given social institution are influenced by the other institutions of the society. The relationship is one of mutual interdependence. The claim of one institution to be fundamental and determinative of the others is rejected because there is no evidence which could be said to count either for or against the claim.

The system of production includes other social institutions than strictly economic ones. Most obvious to a world concerned with raising the standard of living of the underdeveloped countries is that economic institutions presuppose a certain type of education. The study of classical Confucianism is less adequate to the creation of a modern economy than is the study of technology. The system of economic production is too obviously dependent upon other social institutions to be regarded as fundamental and others as derivative. The confusion caused in Marxist circles by focusing on economic interests to the neglect of political interests has been particularly apparent. In short, there is no necessity to treat the system of production as fundamental in Marx's sense.

2. Marx is not clear on his concept of alienation. For Marx, apparently, all people are alienated. If this is so, we have no way of comparing the alienated person with the unalienated person or of knowing exactly what difference alienation makes. To understand alienation, a concept of the unalienated person is needed. Occasionally Marx writes as if the savage were free from alienation, but the bulk of his writing does not permit one to regard Marx's goal as a simple return to nature.

Alienation still bears the marks of its theological origin in Hegel. The doctrine of the fall in theology has at least a formal advantage over Marx's doctrine of alienation. Theology presupposes an essence of humanity and regards humanity in its existence as fallen. Therefore when the theologian is asked how the fallen person compares with the unfallen person, he can point to Jesus, the second Adam, and reply, "Here is the true person."

This approach has difficulties, but at least formally it avoids Marx's dilemma. Marx could find a way out by pointing to the unalienated person of the future and showing how that person will differ from the alienated person of pre-revolution history. But this defense does not carry the same weight as the theologian's claim to point to an historical figure. Positing a perfect person in the future to show what it means to be imperfect in history seems unsatisfyingly circular. For a theoretician who has devalued faith, Marx has left a good deal to the realm of the future and blind faith. His doctrine of alienation encourages a utopianism more thorough-going than religion's dream of otherworldly bliss. Theology, when it has known what it was about, has insisted on an ahistorical fall. The fall was not caused by anything in history which could be remedied. Humanity in its existence is fallen and, though there is salvation in part now, final deliverance is beyond history. Marx, on the other hand, had no illusions about heaven, treated the fall as historical, thought the historical causes could be removed, and had illusions about the future. A more profound type of social criticism will treat alienation as a symbolic representation of humanity's movement from essence to existence, reflecting human freedom over and therefore unhappiness with the world, and then focus more concretely upon the specific ills of our contemporary civilization to correct them where they can be corrected.

3. Even if one is predisposed to accept Marx's contention that religion is the product of humanity as are all his other social institutions, this does not lead to the conclusion that religion is best described as a product of alienation, class ideology, opium of the people, knowledge substitute or a combination of the above. Nor is the conclusion that religion is the product of humanity necessarily an "irreligious criticism." Christian theologians have usually regarded other religions as the products of

humanity. They are coming to regard their own religion similarly, though in varying degrees, insisting that, though religion is a human product, it points symbolically to the eternal or infinite. Sociologists of religion have become more reluctant to describe the origins of religion and more content to analyze its various expressions. Before the enthusiasm for explaining the origins of religion declined, however, several rival explanations were propounded, including views which focused on totemism, animism, magic, the projection of the father image, etc. The origins of religion currently are hidden in a confusion of conflicting opinions; the wise option today is to say with Marx, "Peace to the Teutonic forest," and to study in detail the historical evidence of the vast conglomeration of expressions called religion. Certainly religion is vastly more complicated than Marx regarded it. Probably it is unwise to depend too heavily upon the insights of one who is trying to explain away the religion he describes. Nor is it wise to attempt to explain a massive social phenomena like religion by emphasizing its peripheral aspects. Marx probably over-emphasized the otherworldliness of Christianity, but it was certainly a peculiar methodological approach to emphasize its otherworldliness and then focus upon its sociological expressions. Other Marxists, Eduard Bernstein particularly, studying the social expressions of Christianity, found much less evidence of its social reactionism than did Marx. Bernstein regarded the religious sects of the Cromwellian revolution as forerunners of the Marxist movement. The treatment of religion as a human phenomena, which is a necessary presupposition of the sociology of religion, does not in itself answer the question as to the reality of the depths of existence which Christian theology claims to plumb.

4. As a philosopher-critic of religion, Marx can claim a respected place in the sociological study of religion. But it is as the founder of a

new political religion that he has been raised to his present eminence. How did such a harsh critic of religion come to found a religion? Such a development seems ironical at first, but the pattern of the emergence of a new religion on the criticism of the old one is familiar. The evolution of Marxism has revealed a thorough hatred of religion and especially Christianity because it has combined the jealousy of a competing religion with the disgust of militant atheism toward religion. It was not Marx the empiricist or scientist who founded the new religion, but Marx the materialist. He regarded his scientific materialism as the philosophy which the proletariat would use to overthrow the capitalist system. "As philosophy finds its material weapon in the proletariat, so the proletariat finds its spiritual weapon in philosophy."[17]

The move from critic of religion to founder of a new religion seems to have taken place through a confusion of empiricism with metaphysical materialism.[18] The metaphysical materialism provided Marx with a world view which he thought empiricism verified. From materialism he deduced self-evident propositions which furnished the structure for the new religious apocalypse. Marx's epistemology is not very clear, but he seems to regard any distinctions between the self as object and the self as knower as potentially idealism. The empirical approach, on the other hand, emphasizes the practical and the material and with an indefinite epistemology favors "reality vis-á-vis the fanciful copies of reality." From this materialism he deduces the structure of the new religion.

> There is no need of any great penetration to see from the teaching of materialism on the original goodness and equal intellectual endowment of men, the omnipotence of experience, habit, and education, and the influence of environment on man, the great significance of industry, the justification of enjoyment, etc., how necessarily materialism is connected with communism and socialism.[19]

From this basis of equating empiricism and materialism and deducing communism, the empirical critic receded and the revolutionary prophet came more and more to the fore. The abhorence of dogma was abandoned and the highly speculative doctrines of the messianic role of the proletariat and the climactic revolution followed by a reign of universal justice were adopted. The validation of these ideas lay in their effect in changing the world. The interests of the revolutionary in changing the world are clear in such a test, but the interests of the student of society are neglected. Certainly most illusions, if acted upon strongly enough, would have some effect upon the world. By such a test the religious dogmas Marx hoped to defeat were true. The point of discussing this revolutionary interest of Marx and the materialistic dogmatism which dominated his thought is to point to the lack of empirical precision in his writing. A truly empirical analysis of the conditions of the nineteenth-century laborer would have seen which of the dehumanizing effects of modern technical civilization are due to the profit motive or the division of labor and to what extent these effects are due to the technical process itself. Though the political religion evolving out of Marx's thought is as potent in the twentieth century as the political religion of Islam was in the seventh, the lack of empirical precision in analyzing the industrial process renders Marx less relevant than he might have been to modern civilization's attempts to relieve the suffering of its people.

Morals in <u>Das Kapital</u>

The reader of <u>Das Kapital</u> cannot escape a sense of moral outrage at the conditions of nineteenth-century capitalism. Marx's analysis of Western economic and social life is also an indictment of the system and a call to overthrow it. Political economy's treatment of the individual as an abstract unit of labor was regarded by Marx as one of its major deficiencies. He

attempted in his writing to break with the tradition of assessing the proletarian as a productive animal and focused also on the laborer's housing,
leisure time, food, quality of cultural life, and potential for fulfilling
the proletarian's human capabilities.

Marx preaches no explicit moral standards in Das Kapital; rather he
reports on the historical situation of the worker and analyzes the economic
evolution and structure of society. The work is avowedly descriptive rather
than normative. But Marx's skill at reporting and quoting others to report
the squalid conditions of labor evoke a normative response in his reader.
His skillful weaving of testimony and analysis is designed to predispose the
reader toward his vision of the economic world divided into two classes, the
exploiters and the exploited. For example, he writes of the struggle of the
proletariat to win back a normal working day:

> In its blind, unbridled passion, its werewolf hunger for
> surplus labor, capital is not content to overstep the moral
> restrictions upon the length of the working day. It over-
> steps the purely physical limitations as well.[20]

Marx quotes the capitalists themselves to reveal their motivation of greed.

For example, in regard to the debate over the hours children should work, the
capitalist accuses himself:

> Our objection to not allowing boys under 18 to work at
> night, would be on account of the increase of expense,
> but this is the only reason.[21]

The moral tone of the work is illustrated by two further examples:

> The "House of Terror" for paupers of which capitalists were
> already dreaming in 1770, came into existence a few years
> later in the shape of a gigantic Workhouse for the industrial
> workers. It was called a factory. The ideal [of the
> capitalists] paled before the reality.[22]

> For protection against the worm gnawing at their vitals,
> the workers must put their heads together, and must as
> a class compel the passing of a law, the erection of an
> all-powerful social barrier, which will forbid even the

workers themselves from entering into a free contract when
by the terms of that contract they and their race are condemned to death or sold into slavery.[23]

Das Kapital documents in hundreds of examples Fawcett's charge that:

> The rich grow rapidly richer, whilst there is no percept-
> ible advance in the comfort enjoyed by the industrial
> classes. . . . They [the workers] become almost the slaves
> of the tradesmen to whom they owe money.[24]

Das Kapital can be regarded as probably the most severe, certainly the most

influential, moral indictment of nineteenth-century capitalism. However, it

avoids moral terminology, and its author had earlier protested against

abstract moralisms.

The German Ideology, jointly authored by Marx and Engels, boldly pro-

claims the death of morality, religion, metaphysics and all other forms of

thought which could be regarded as ideology. But the proclamation in The

German Ideology that "Communists preach no morality at all" reveals only one

side of Marx's thought on morals from 1848 to 1883; the break with the

younger moralist Marx is less complete than a superficial reading of The

German Ideology might lead one to conclude.

Das Kapital evokes a moral response in its reader because it combines

implicit moral judgments with a description of a situation which evokes a

moral judgment. It is not necessary for Das Kapital to present a formal

framework of moral standards; the reader brings one's own framework of moral

principles plus one's own experiences with the productive process to the read-

ing of the situation described. Moral philosophers who regard themselves as

nondescriptivists are often today ready to concede that a moral judgment does

involve descriptive as well as prescriptive judgments. Marx provides the

descriptive judgments in his "scientific" critique of political economy and,

though he relies on the reader's own prescriptive judgments to evoke a moral judgment in the context, he also smuggles in normative judgments. The above quotations disclose moral passion as well as scientific description in the metaphorical comparison of a factory to a workhouse, in the description of a desire for profits as a "werewolf hunger," in the use of "must" in the sense of a hypothetical imperative and in the reference to the violation of "moral restrictions."

According to Marx's analysis, nineteenth-century capitalism was destined to die; furthermore, it deserved its death through the eventual rise of the proletariat and violent revolution because it violated humanity's freedom and social harmony. Capitalism, and the bourgeois morality it nourished, reduced people to competing atomic individuals who could neither cooperate as species beings nor fulfill themselves as individuals. The lack of cooperation and common aims prevented one from attaining true human dignity and stifled the chance to be free. It is this dual violation of humanity which resounds through the pages of Das Kapital; humanity does not cooperate, and is in slavery. The lack of cooperation is often portrayed in terms which speak of the illogical nature of the productive process under capitalism. Marx's hatred of all which bound humanity provides the source of an anecdote quoted by E. H. Carr:

> Twenty years after that, when one of his daughters handed him
> a Victorian questionnaire asking him, inter alia, to state
> the vice he detested most, he wrote Servility.[25]

Robert C. Tucker points to 1843-1847 as the period of transmigration from Marx the moralist and philosopher into Marx the revolutionary. It was in this period that he drew upon Lorenz von Stein's report to shape the role of the proletariat as the bearers of the revolution. Also the economic implications of Hegelianism became more clearly delineated.[26] Marx's earlier use of alienation gave way to the discussion of the division of labor.

Division of labor in _Das Kapital_ seems to serve the same function as alienation in _Economic and Philosophical Manuscripts_ and earlier writings. The
discussion of the capitalist system, therefore, is a continuation of Marx's
analysis of alienated man. It is this move from alienation of labor (which
is obvious once the division of labor is recognized as the source of alienation) that provides an implicit moral structure for the analysis of the capitalist system. Karl Popper, who is not centrally concerned with alienation,
has written, "Marx's condemnation of capitalism is fundamentally a moral condemnation."[27] Consideration of Marx's use of alienation illuminates the
implicit morality of _Das Kapital_ while pointing to bourgeois morality as a
symptom of alienation.

Bourgeois Morality

Engels' _Anti-Duhring_ captures one side of Marx's teaching on morality.
It expresses the rejection of moralists' claims to eternal truth and reduces
morality to a class consciousness. Engels regards three moralities as of
importance in Western Europe: (1) Christian with feudal overtones, (2) bourgeois with elements of Christian ethics, and (3) the proletarian morality.
The three moralities have some common elements due to their sharing a common
historical background, but none of them are true in the sense of having absolute validity. Engels regards all of them as serving to justify the systems
of production which they reflect. The proletarian morality "contains the
maximum of durable element" because it represents the interests of the class
which will overthrow the present structure and survive in the future.[28] Marx
and Engels shared the tendency of lightly dismissing moral or religious arguments against their theories. Ideological arguments often obscured the
central areas of conflict, which were over the system of production.

Engels may never have appreciated the full depth of Karl Marx's attack on bourgeois morality. Marx's attack on bourgeois morality was in part, also, an attack on moralism or on heteronomous morality. He shared with Kant a conception of the moral life which valued the individual's own free adoption of one's principles. Ethics which recognize sanctions from higher powers (whether they be the state, gods, or social standards) are coercive and express one's alienated essence over against oneself. Kamenka regards this criticism of morality as of fundamental importance to the young Marx.

> This is an ethical criticism. Moralism, the postulation of rights and duties and the application of legal punishments and sanctions seeks to bind men from outside. They are therefore forms of bondage and not of freedom. As such they cannot produce freedom. This we may remember, was his criticism of Hegel's conception of a coercive State that was nevertheless "the rational form of freedom." These things in their coercion, are evils and cannot be productive of goods.[29]

This perspective of Marx's attack on heteronomous morality clarifies the paradox of his moral condemnation of capitalism combined with his rejection of morality. Marx's attack on morality may be better described as an attack upon "moralism."

Marx also found repugnant the attacks upon the unfortunate in society, the outcast. Too much effort was spent condemning the unfortunates and not enough in trying to understand them. Marx shared the tendency of much of the most progressive moral thinking to explain human actions rather than to judge them. "Man," he wrote, "seems a mystery to man: one knows only how to blame him, there is no knowledge of him."[30] However, Marx's tendency in his later writings to hide his moral judgments under "scientific" description coupled with his attack on morality as class ideology permitted his followers to slide easily into viewing morality as correlated with technical, economic and scientific progress. Some of the values which Marx himself most wanted

to uphold came to be neglected by his disciples, partly because of his lack
of explicit discussion of the moral issues in his later writings.

The Essence of Marxian Morality

The heart of Marx's morality is hidden in his earlier writings under
his Marxian-Hegelian metaphysic and in his later writings under his critique
of political economy. However the two themes of human cooperation and freedom which dominate his writing are perennial issues in moral philosophy.
Marx had little hope that the competition of atomic units would produce the
greatest good for all. He regarded the competitive rush for consumption as
creating discord in society. Anarchic competition resulted in people being
used by the masters as means to never-satisfied ends. His hope for a "kingdom of ends" may be utopian, but his focus on the value of cooperation or
harmony is in the tradition of great moral philosophy. The second value
praised most highly by Marx was freedom. Marx was a determinist, however;
he did not regard ethics as dependent upon freedom of the will. Rather for
him freedom meant ability to be determined from within and to fulfill human
potential in accord with the laws of one's own being. The values of vitality,
sincerity, spontaneous cooperation,and capacity for production are regarded
by Marx as more truly human than avarice, anxiety, and the search for security.

Marx's attack on Eugene Sue reveals his idea of a completely unre-
pressive morality. The adults of Marx's new society, apparently, are to
live in mutual forebearance, each serving the other's ends while fulfilling
one's own. The Kantian idea of a moral obligation seems to be replaced in
Marx's ethic with a goal of a holy will. Marx's ethic is not so much designed
to change society as it is to change human nature.

> The abstraction of the political man was very well described
> by Rousseau: He who dares undertake to give instructions to
> a nation ought to feel himself capable of changing human
> nature; of transforming every individual who in himself is a
> complete and independent whole into part of a greater whole,
> from which he receives in some manner his life and his being;
> of altering man's constitution in order to strengthen it.[31]

For Marx, the classless society is an association of "truly human men" or

"all-round individuals." The individual would not be free in the bourgeois

sense, but in the Hegelian-Marxian sense in which needs are at the same time

social needs and to whom "freedom is the appreciation of necessity."

Negation of Negation

Das Kapital assumes the character of the communist society without

demonstrating it in detail. Engels was more prone than Marx to outline the

new society. For Marx, communism was a society of human dignity in which

property had been overcome and production was controlled by the free associa-

tion of producers.

Economic and Philosophical Manuscripts describes the various stages

of the evolution of communism. The first stage is one of negation in which

the old social order is destroyed in a class war. Marx regarded the class

war as an inevitability which was demonstrable through an analysis of the

structure of capitalism. He regarded himself as participating in the con-

flict and could not have been unaware of his own role in sharpening the class

consciousness of the proletariat. He described the social structure in terms

of the two great antagonists whose ultimate conflict approached as the prole-

tariat increased in numbers and class consciousness. In Marx's thought the

developing class consciousness was both a historical reality and a necessity

for the sake of the social revolution. The description and prescription

merged in Marx's vision of the class revolution that ought to be and was taking place. In the <u>Communist</u> <u>Manifesto</u> he wrote:

> Our epoch, the epoch of the bourgeoisie, possesses, however,
> this distinctive feature; it has simplified the class antagon-
> isms. Society as a whole is more and more splitting up into
> two great hostile camps, into two great classes directly
> facing each other--bourgeoisie and proletariat.[32]

This historical development correlated nicely with the necessities of the

revolution which Marx had recognized through his study of the French revo-

lution:

> For one class to be the liberating class <u>par excellence</u> it
> is essential that another class should be openly the oppress-
> ing class. The negative significance of the French nobility
> and clergy produced the positive significance of the
> bourgeoisie the class which stood next to them and opposed
> them.[33]

The first destructive stage of communism will eliminate everything

that cannot be shared by all. It will possess a negative character due to

its birth in capitalism and its first results will be to destroy the rights

which previously only a few men had enjoyed. People will not escape their

alienation in this early destructive period of communism. It is a negative

period in which all people are reduced to the same level, but new opportuni-

ties for self-affirmation will not be developed. This first stage of commun-

ism is to be brief, and people are expected to outgrow their capitalist pas-

sions, but Marx fails to provide convincing reasons why those in this stage

will outgrow their egoistic drives. Perhaps the change in the system of pro-

duction is expected to change humanity, but Marx does not make clear how the

changes he envisages in the first stage will produce a mankind capable of

progress to further stages. It is hard to conceive of this "infinite degrada-

tion" being the beginning of Marx's radical reform of mankind. Marx saw more

clearly than many the cost of social change and the destruction that class

warfare would entail. But he failed to reconcile the revolution with the new

mankind he hoped would emerge.

Tucker believes that Marx's failure to escape the dilemma of the negation of the negation reveals the weakness of his moral thought.

> The moral escapism at the core of Marx's thought finds expression, finally, in this conception of the means of self-change. Collectivizing the process and evading the issue of individual responsibility for self-liberation, he ended up by invoking one set of destructive passions to destroy another. Dispossessed by capital of his productive powers, dehumanized man was to be motivated by wrath, hatred, envy and greed in the war to reappropriate them. . . . There could be no greater confession of failure on Marx's part than this mode of envisagement of the old moral revolution of self-change that he had postulated as the goal for man.[34]

There is a weakness in Marx's writing on the first stage of communism, but given the class analysis of Marxism and the resistance of the bourgeoisie something like the destruction and leveling which Marx discussed seems consistent. Marx's failure is not in recommending the leveling or negation process, but in failing to demonstrate that an unalienated person could evolve through such a process. A more utopian Marx might have found a way for the new person to emerge from the negation process; a less utopian Marx might never have expected the emergence of an unalienated one.

Critique of Marx's Ethic

Karl Marx's morality is a critical morality. It exposed the grossness of what many regarded as a Christian industrial order in mid-nineteenth-century Europe. It provided a vision of the "laughing young lions" or those truly free people who would build a new order. The vision was fuller than the program. The morality of Marx has been mixed with various other forces which on the one hand take the movements of social reform out of the thrust of organized religious movements and on the other hand are captured by totalitarian political machines with their own religious overtones. The positive contribution of Marx to moral reflection has been to challenge fundamentally the illusion that a brutal capitalism was morally tolerable. He enabled many to see the extent to which their so-called moral principles were, instead, an ideology for the protection of their own place in the economic system. A discussion of Marx's moral philosophy is not complete, however, until some of its serious deficiencies have been mentioned.

1. Marx has not successfully demonstrated that morals are wholly determined by economic conditions or social structures. Nor has he adequately indicated what would count as evidence for and against his assertion. To suggest that Aristotle had a bias in favor of slavery is not to prove that his whole ethic was determined by the Athenian system of production. Nor does reference to the production systems of fifth-century Athens explain the different moral views held by Athenian citizens represented in Plato's dialogues. Marx's insight that philosophy is influenced by the passions and needs of the philosophers is a valuable contribution, but he has not convincingly argued that morality is only a reflection of the system of production.

2. Marx's attacks on bourgeois concepts of liberty, which meant liberty only for the strong, were well-founded. But his tendency toward determinism vitiated his moral teaching. The issues between determinism and free will cannot be resolved in a few sentences, but the conflicts between Augustine and Pelagius, Luther and Erasmus, the Calvinists and Wesley point to the church's inability to maintain a consistent determinism even in a mysterious providential form. An economic determinism, which is much more specific than a providential determinism, is even more threatening to moral responsibility. Of course, forms of determinism (Islam, Calvinism, and Marxism) produce very moral adherents, but they are not internally consistent. Their activist policies and advocacy styles belie their confidence that the

sorting out of the sheep and the goats has already been determined. Freedom
for these deterministic systems means full participation within the system,
not the ability to influence an undecided future. Denying the ability to
influence an undecided future excludes an element of fundamental importance
from the doctrine of humanity. Marx's whole metaphysic blinded him to the
possibilities of seeing freedom within history and encouraged him to postu-
late it as a goal of history.

3. Marx's morality is not an adequate substitute for the tradition
of Western moral philosophy because it ignores so many of the classical issues
of moral philosophy. The problems of the connections between freedom and responsibility; the relationship between rights and duty; the definition of the
good; analysis of conscience; the conflict between social interest and family
interest; the discussion of virtues and vices; the relationship between
descriptive and prescriptive judgments are human problems which need illumi-
nation. Marx's awareness of the corruption of morality by interest is a valuable deepening of Western ethical reflection, but he ignores too many problems
to serve as the cornerstone of a new moral philosophy.

4. Marx's attempt to reduce morality to class consciousness meant
that ethics was surrendered to the political program of the proletariat.
When the proletariat's inability to lead moved Lenin to substitute the party
for the proletariat as the vanguard of the revolution, ethics was subsumed
under the political program of the party. This result, which in the Soviet
Union has produced a vigorous work morality, is a form of the heteronomous
morality which Marx had attacked. The Calvinist work morality and the Soviet
work morality are not structurally very different, though they serve different
classes. The norms of ethics which Marx did not defend are reduced in Soviet
society to the political program of those in power.

   5. Despite the beauty of particular passages in which Marx describes
the future unalienated person, his vision of the truly human is not clear.
The unalienated person is one who will have fulfilled his capacities as a
social being. However, as Professor John Plamenatz has indicated, the precise
meaning of such fulfillment is not clear. There are many different capacities
a person or a society could fulfill; to choose one way is to deny other routes
to satisfaction. If Marx means people would choose to be contented, there are
different ways in which people could be contented. If Marx means humanity
would develop to the point where it would choose the admirable, the question
arises, which view of the admirable will be accepted? Marx often writes as
if the unalienated person will be the amateur who is free to choose to engage
in productive or recreational activities as one wills. But the vision of the
amateur as the fulfilled person is being seriously questioned today. Excellence often requires specialization. Excellence in art, work, or play can be
a great source of satisfaction and certainly cannot be eliminated from any
concept of human fulfillment. This deliberate parallel of his theory of revolution to the Christian hope shows that, at least at times, he was partially
conscious of the similarities between his eschatology and some Christian
eschatology. Probably, though, the degree to which his entire philosophy of
history was honeycombed by religious assumptions remained hidden from this
philosopher who so hated religion. From the perspective of the twentieth
century, both eschatologies seem to have been less than complete, but our
study of politics is enriched by the suggestion of practical power that trust
in an eschatological vision engenders.

On Revolution

The previous exposition and critique of Marx's positions on religion and morality lead to the conclusion that, in his perspective, neither way of coping with historical existence was adequate. The questions raised about his conclusions suggest that his own perspective was incomplete. However, his thought on religion and morals was set in the context of his own thought about revolution. If a thinker is committed to a perspective that an apocalyptic revolution is near, it follows that all forms of life which relate to the present epoch are doomed. Given Marx's apocalyptic perspective, his discontent with nineteenth century institutions is as inevitable as early Christian discontent with Roman society and mores.

In a sense, his whole thought is about the social revolution, and the philosophical reflections, economic theory and writing about the travails of 1848 and 1871 are all of a piece. The scholarly debate and the newly translated manuscripts of the Grundrisse establish this continuity beyond a doubt.[35]

Marx's general theory of revolution is best seen in the manifesto he and Engels drew up in 1848 at the request of the Communist League. In the preface to The Communist Manifesto, Engels attributes the fundamental concept of the document to Marx. This central thesis of their joint writing is in essence the Marxist theory of revolution. The history of mankind is that of class struggles resulting from the contradictions within the system of economic production and at the present time the proletariat is engaged in the final struggle to overthrow the bourgeoisie. With the victory of the proletariat the end of the struggles is in sight and consequently the end to exploitation and oppression. The system of production and distribution is fundamental. Those who control the system of production control the state and the centers of ideological influence. Marx is not primarily concerned with equality of distribution, but with the rational utilization of the system of production for human welfare.

Human history is a bloody record, "a slaughter bench" of class struggles, in which a pattern of evolution can be seen. The victory of the bourgeois revolutions (e.g., the French revolution) has prepared a stage in which the power of the exploited is increasing as they are impoverished, and the power of the exploiter is decreasing as they increase their wealth and decrease in numbers.

The argument of The Communist Manifesto calls for revolutionary struggle which will shift power to the working class, but it does so in the context of seeing the push of historical forces to this goal. For Marx, not ideals but the fundamental forces of history are bringing about the changes which result in revolution.

The dynamics of the bourgeois system of production drove people eventually even out of the ranks of production. It reduced workers to paupers and, because it increased misery so unbearably for others, the opposition against it would continue to rise. The new system of production also pushed workers into association, and within the workers' association breathed, or so Marx believed, "revolutionary combination." In the political language of the Manifesto, the bourgeois-dominated society was producing its own gravediggers and its fall was inevitable.

The immediate aims of the Communist Party are presented as synonymous with the aims of the proletariat itself and also with other proletarian parties. The vagueness regarding precisely who are the Communists in relationship to the proletariat contains the seeds of Marx's own tendency toward anarchism and also the tendency expressed by Lenin toward personal dictatorship in the name of the proletariat. This fundamental ambivalence in Marxist

theory is seen even in contemporary Soviet literature. Mikhail Sholokhov
in And Quiet Flows the Don represents both the revolutionary cossacks and
the Bolsheviks as being quite vague about who will control Russia after the
revolution. Both groups, however, were quite clear as to the fundamental
nature of Communist revolution being, as Marx had described it, "the most
radical rupture with traditional property relations."[36] The rupture of the
system of property tears asunder the structures and ideas which had legitimated the previous epoch.

Marx is quite clear that the first battle of the workers' revolution
is to gain political control. The second step is to strip capital from the
bourgeoisie. Centralization of control of the means of production follows,
and steps are to be taken to increase the productivity of the economic system under its new proletarian management. Specific reforms will vary from
country to country, but generally Marx's goal was to increase the possibilities of free human development through tearing down structures of oppression
and replacing them with welfare structures, e.g., free education in public
schools, etc.

These changes cannot take place in Marx's opinion without the sweep-
ing away of the present political orders. "Political power, properly so
called, is merely the organized power of one class for oppressing another."[37]
The ending of oppression requires the elimination of the oppressors and,
though the focus is not on violence, it is assumed that violence is a necessary tool for change. Violence is assumed to be part of the historical
matrix, and the Communist gains "can be attained only by the forcible overthrow of all existing social conditions."[38] The unique Communist contribution to the turmoil of Europe in the mid-nineteenth century was, to Marx and
Engels, its continual focus on the property question and the encouragement

of proletarian antagonism against the bourgeoisie even though temporary
alliances might be necessary.

The elements of vision and hope are very strong in this militant
document. Although Marx disparages utopian socialists and other groups, he
does not attack them as severely for their ideals as he does for their failure to understand the disruptive changes the whole society must go through to
produce the new community where one can be free. Apparently his vision is
one of the elimination of political power, the end of all oppression, and "the
free development of all."[39] The controversy over the utopian elements in
Marx's theory of the revolution of society is widespread. Reinhold Niebuhr[40]
regards the fanaticism of Marxian utopianism as perhaps the chief weakness
of Marxist thought which is traceable to Marx himself. On the other hand,
Robert C. Tucker[41] regards the utopian elements of vision as the single greatest contribution of Marx to the solution of the dilemmas of today, whereas
Niebuhr finds the illusions of utopianism a distraction from the solutions to
contemporary problems. The issues of the Christian-Marxist dialogue cannot
be resolved without a conclusion to the question of the appropriateness of
Marx's own apocalypticism or utopianism.

Marx's thoughts on revolution in its immediate political sense are
best represented in his The Civil War in France. Previous to the uprising
in Paris against the Provisional Government and its Prussian allies, Marx had
warned against the folly of armed rebellion. He urged the workers to expand
their own work through the offices of the republic. When Paris arose on
March 18, 1871, to the cries of "Vive la Commune!" Marx supported the efforts
of the Parisians to determine their own destiny. In a letter to Dr. Dugelmann
on the events in Paris, he revealed his own strong sense for the role accident
plays in history. The accidents did not, he assumed, finally alter the

general course of historical development, but they were very important in
accelerating or delaying the movement of history. It was not, he thought,
the general conditions of French society which frustrated the revolution of
the commune, but rather it was the presence of the Prussian army which was
decisive. The alteration in Marx's position on the commune strikes the
interested but non-true-believer as indicating that: Marx did not know when
revolutionary movements might succeed; he was willing to urge caution and
coalition when other communists were ready to use force; he could be dragged
into causes in which he might not at first choose to commit himself; and his
overall theory included the recognition that historical contingency was
determinative in particular cases.

The defeated commune was the model until 1917 for Marxist theory as
to what a revolution looked like. Engels, taunting social democrats who
were afraid of the dictatorship of the proletariat, would write: "Well and
good, gentlemen, do you want to know what this dictatorship looks like?
Look at the Paris Commune. That was the Dictatorship of the Proletariat."[42]

For Marx the martyred defenders of the commune had begun the communist program for the new society even if they were limited by their time, their
fighting for their lives, and their Blanquist and Proudhonist presuppositions.
The program that he applauded had begun the disestablishment of the churches;
reorganization of the government with universal suffrage, directed representatives, recall, reduced salaries; suppression of the army; organization of
militia; freeing of education; expropriation of property; stopping of rents;
reforming working patterns; and other elements of the communist revolution.
Marx exulted in the decline in crime and the general cleansing of the city
of the patterns of life associated with bourgeois decadence. He also noted
how soon the prostitutes, drunkenness, etc., returned to Paris with the

victory of the Versailles army and the return of bourgeois life.

As a revolutionary, Marx's allies and comrades were destroyed in the holocaust. As an interpreter he secured the meaning of the Paris Commune in words which were to inspire generations of later-day, left-wing revolutionaries, including Lenin, who "declared that the young Soviet Republic stood on the shoulders of the Paris Commune."[43]

Marx regarded the revolutions which ended historical epochs as important, but these political revolutions were not as central to his thought as were the broader social revolutions. Lenin, as a theorist of revolution, focused much more on the particulars of political-national revolutions than did Marx. Marx, by Leninist standards, is more of a meta-revolutionary. He is not thinking primarily of the revolution of Germans or Russians but of the revolution of the human species. Revolution for Marx is a salvation concept, his history is salvation history, and on the other side of the communist revolution he expects a new man, an emerging progressive humanism without government.

On many particular matters Marx was a man of his own time. His judgments about the inevitable developments of capitalism, for example, have often been criticized. The merging of Lenin's understanding of revolution with Marx's has made the Marxist concepts of revolution the primary source of revolutionary theory in the third world. The power of Marx's analysis in the West has been an important factor in humanizing the system of production and distribution and in consequently reducing the appeal of revolution among the proletariat. Of course, the proletariat themselves have been changed by the economic changes. The continued visibility of some aspects of Marxian analysis is demonstrated in the resurgence of Marxian history, in the ideological-left activist groups, within the everyday work in social theory in classrooms, writing and public discussion, and within the churches as the Christian-Marxist dialogue is taken seriously. With all the problems a Marxist revolutionary understanding contains, the question remains of whether there is an alternative body of theory with equivalent persuasive power. However, at the heart of his thought is an idea of an anti-kingdom, a society without government. Such an anti-kingdom picture is a useful weapon for ideological critique of all existing institutions, but it may not be as useful for helping people to find ways of ordering their societies justly.

Marxism has branched many revisionist forms of understanding from its founder's complex thought. The purpose of this study is not to follow them, but to examine a movement of social-reform Christianity in the United States, which utilized some aspects of Marxism, to look at Christian realism which became strongly anti-Marxist in the pressures of the cold war, and finally to reflect on how theologians of hope and revolution are returning to many of Marx's central concerns. The attempt is to show how, in all these movements, their eschatology was correlated with and supportive of their politics. The goal is to distill elements which will enrich contemporary thinking about a world experiencing revolutions.

V. CHRISTIAN SOCIALISM AND THE KINGDOM OF GOD

Fundamental to the task of changing society is a sense of basic trust in the way things are or are going to become. Hope in a better order grows out of a sense that things can and will be better. This hope has historically had a religious base. Even in the faith of Marxism the religious undergirding of the hope is evident. The antireligious establishment of the Enlightenment also revealed a religious quality in their hopes for mankind.

This quality of hope for a new order often has its origins in a sense that God wills righteousness, and the present order is unrighteous. The prophetic and apocalyptic traditions of Hebrew faith reflect this confidence that God will judge His people and then deliver them. The hope here is in God's decisive action in the future to right the present wrongs. Jesus continues this movement, and just as his sense of God's righteousness demands eschatological fulfillment, so his sense of the coming of the Kingdom shapes his ethic. The movement is a dialectical one. The apocalyptic traditions carry with them their own persuasive power and insure that they will influence perceptions of what it is fitting to do in a history under judgment. Also at work is the conviction that God's rule is to be fulfilled, justice is to be done, and that conviction demands some sort of eschatological fulfillment because it cannot happen in history as presently endured.

In America, the motif of the Kingdom of God had been central to the religious consciousness of the people. It had sustained various interpretations. H. Richard Niebuhr's study[1] showed how American movements of renewal in the church could be characterized as different interpretations of the Kingdom of God.

During the period of approximately fifty years after 1880, a movement which became labeled as the social gospel emphasized the Kingdom of God as a coming rule of God over humanity. Social gospellers maintained the other meanings of the Kingdom also, but its central meaning was upon the expected rule of God in a commonwealth. This hope demanded a redirection of life now, and they bent their efforts to reshaping the institutional life of America. The movement came to dominate the seminaries, major pulpits, newspapers, social service agencies of the northern churches, but it did not control the grass roots population of the church's mind. It rode with the progressive thought of the secular world in its day and, though growing out of the evangelical revivals, its thought was heavily influenced by European liberal theology.

The social strategies of the social gospel movement included the whole spectrum from Christian social welfare work to Christian communism and various types of Christian communal societies. The center of the movement was dominated by a mild form of Christian socialism which called for structural changes in society. This group focused particularly on the evils of the economic system and moved from proposals of reform of capitalism to the deplacement of capitalism by various types of socialism. In articulating Christian socialist answers, the reformers were conscious of standing in a Christian socialist tradition much older than Karl Marx. Often the hopes of the social gospel leaders were not much different in detail from the hopes of various communist or socialist leaders. However, the social gospel leaders of the center were characterized by a reluctance to use armed force for social change and, in many cases, by pacifism. Probably in their analysis their sense of the great injustices of capitalism and their refusal to use armed force to change the order collided. Yet armed force was not a relevant strategy in

late nineteenth or early twentieth-century America. If they did refuse to
see how realistically some of the Biblical prophets which they quoted taught
that only divine intervention and the forceful smashing of an order could be
the grounds for a new order, they did remain consistent with the pacifism they
found in Jesus' teaching in the gospels.

Evolution was, for many of the articulate of the social gospel movement, the bridge between the present reality of injustice and the ideal of
the brotherhood of man under God's rule. Others stressed the movement of God
more, but generally speaking the social gospel emphasized the partnership of
God and humanity in realizing the Kingdom of God. If orthodox Christianity
has for twenty centuries refused to delineate or separate God and humanity in
Jesus Christ's actions, the writers of social gospel theology could be permitted some ambiguity on this relationship in the transformation of the republic
into the Kingdom of God.

Standing in the center of the social gospel theologians is Walter
Rauschenbusch, who is generally regarded as the movement's most brilliant
spokesman. Rauschenbusch was the son of a German immigrant pastor. He himself was pastor in Hell's Kitchen, New York City, until reduced hearing and
the opportunity of teaching lured him away from the pastorate to teach at his
own seminary in Rochester, New York. His education, his pastorate and his
teaching had all been both in English and German, and he combined in himself
the social passion for reform of the new country with the depth of theological inquiry of his father's homeland. A consideration of two of his major
themes, the Kingdom of God and the critique of capitalism, reveals the essence
of his social theology.

The Kingdom of God

Walter Rauschenbusch's theology was organized around one central idea, and he taught that the preserved teaching of Jesus also emphasized the Kingdom of God as its central motif. C. Howard Hopkins has caught the spirit of this conception in Rauschenbush by quoting him:

> In the Alps I have seen the summit of some great mountain come
> out of the clouds in the early morning and stand revealed in
> blazing purity. Its foot was still swathed in drifting mist,
> but I knew the mountain was there and my soul rejoiced in it.
> So Christ's conception of the Kingdom of God came to me as a
> new revelation. Here was the idea and purpose that had domi-
> nated the mind of the Master himself. All his teachings
> center about it. His life was given to it. His death was
> suffered for it. When a man has once seen that in the gospels,
> he can never unsee it again.[2]

From Rauschenbusch's earliest writing to his last, he set his theology and his sociology in the perspective of the Kingdom. During World War I, he set even that event, which ended nineteenth-century Europe, in the perspective of the coming Kingdom. He stated, in his prayers, the hope for the coming Kingdom as he blended the highest devotional life with a polemic against capitalism. Referring to the opening petitions of the Lord's Prayer, he wrote:

> They look forward to the ultimate perfection of the common
> life of humanity on this earth, and pray for the divine revo-
> lution which is to bring that about.[3]

In a prayer entitled "For the Cooperative Commonwealth," thanking God that the vision of peace could now be turned into reality, he prayed:

> Speed now the day when the plains and the hills and the
> wealth thereof shall be the people's own, and thy freemen
> shall not live as tenants of men on the earth which thou
> hast given to all; when no babe shall be born without its
> equal birthright in the riches and knowledge wrought out by
> the labor of the ages; and when the mighty engines of
> industry shall throb with a gladder music because the men
> who ply these great tools shall be their owners and masters.[4]

A step beyond the recognition that Rauschenbusch believed the reformation of the church and the true preaching of the gospel required the

rediscovery of the doctrine of the Kingdom of God, is the inquiry into the
meaning of the doctrine. Admittedly, some ambiguity can be tolerated for
religious language does not often speak univocally about its ultimate references. However, the greatest degree of clarity possible is required for a
judgment about the continuing usefulness of the concept of which he wrote,
"The doctrine is itself the social gospel."[5]

The Kingdom of God was first, for Rauschenbusch, the reality of which
Jesus preached. It was the old hope of a messianic theocracy in Israel which
Jesus changed in the direction of universality, spirituality, non-forceful
means of fulfillment, and elevation of the value of personhood.[6] The Kingdom's goal was the conversion of every human life into its full potential and
the restructuring of all human institutions of life so that they met human
needs.[7] The awareness of the Kingdom was initiated by Jesus, and it has been
the mission of the church to announce its reality and to labor for its fulfillment.

The clearest statement of its contemporary meaning is found in the
last of Rauschenbusch's books, A Theology for the Social Gospel. In this
statement in which he attempts to organize systematically his theological
position, he presents the Kingdom as a movement within history which is detec-
ted by religious sensitivity. The movement has both prescriptive and descriptive qualities. History is seen as the human story which contains within
it negative and positive tendencies. The Kingdom is those positive tendencies
which are also the qualities which fulfill human life or, to use theological
language, realize a "social incarnation of God." "The Kingdom of God is
history seen in a religious and teleological way."[8]

In the chapter, "The Kingdom of God," he lists eight propositions
which he argues are a basis for the theology of the Kingdom. Five of the

propositions treat the Kingdom as the goal of God or of human fulfillment.
The words "end" and teleology are central in this presentation. Clearly in
this understanding, history is considered to be moving in a direction, and
ethics becomes the inquiry as to how to act to help realize that goal. However, the Kingdom is not only future, it is a movement with a past, it is a
reality in the present to the extent that human life is congruous with its
final end, and its fulfillment will be in an unknown future. The Kingdom "is
the energy of God realizing itself in human life."[9] The fulfillment is, of
course, for Rauschenbusch, in God's control, but as God realizes Himself in
human loving action and as the unity of God and humanity is the highest religious conception, to affirm God's government of the Kingdom is not to deny
humanity. The Kingdom, for Rauschenbusch, contains within itself the ideas
of immanence and transcendence, and they are held in balance.

Christianity for Rauschenbusch is a permanent revolution, and the
Kingdom of God is the goal of the revolution. The efforts of all contribute
to the movement of history, but some have discerned the goal of history,
Christian discernment coming through Jesus and the church, and they act more
helpfully. The time of the victory is not known, but Rauschenbusch shows dis-
dain for all theories which act to postpone action on its behalf. The Kingdom
is the zest of life and, by accepting it and working for it, the Christian
finds his home.

Max Stackhouse's attempt to present the logic of Rauschenbusch's
position stresses the predominant eschatological quality of the Kingdom.[10]
The eschatology is of the character that stresses continuity between the signs
in the present of God's redemptive work and His fulfillment. However, in
interpreting the historical manifestations of the Kingdom, he focuses on its
ideational, natural and institutional expressions. In this interpretation

Stackhouse is trying to get beneath Rauschenbusch's own writing to the system. Rauschenbusch's own tendency to speak about the development of the idea, its relevance, and its effects avoids the dangers of this tendency to over-systematize a generally non-systematic thinker. The _ideational_ and _institutional_ dimensions are present, but they are not on a comparable level which permits them to be seen as complementary categories. The _natural_ dimension does not seem to be prominent in Rauschenbusch's thought about the Kingdom, though perhaps in a day of ecological crisis it would be a desirable dimension. Also the presence of the natural dimension, as in the case of the lion and the lamb lying down together, would have helped to free Rauschenbusch from the misplaced charges of easy optimism. Rather, it seems that the qualities Stackhouse regarded as natural were simply the somewhat commonplace organic metaphors which were used to interpret society. Similarly, Stackhouse stretches a point when he interprets Rauschenbusch's early enthusiasm for Henry George's land tax as indicating a priority in his system for a dimension of nature in the Kingdom of God. Stackhouse asserts that "Land is the root metaphor for Rauschenbusch's understanding of the economic system. Land is the primary means of production."[11] It is true that Rauschenbusch did not articulate a labor theory of value, but it is also true that he regarded possession of land as a source of wealth first as real estate in cities and then as a source of raw materials as only two of five ways that great riches were amassed in the twentieth century. His critique of political economy[12] for ignoring the human dimension of economics, and his insistence that political economy needed to be anthropocentric, leads in an opposite direction from Stackhouse's contention that land was primary in his economic thinking.[13] In the human use or misuse of resources and not in the resources themselves rests the connections with the Kingdom of God.

The above disagreement with Stackhouse's analysis of Rauschenbusch's position does not imply disagreement with his major thesis: "The ways in which the concepts of history and the Kingdom of God function in Rauschenbusch contain elements of continuing validity."[14] The new enthusiasm for the theology of hope emphasis points to the need for expression within social theologies of resources which will encourage the transformation of the historical realities of human life as well as the understanding of the conditions of that life.

Christian Socialism

Rauschenbusch was no less critical of capitalism than his Marxist contemporaries. He saw that Christian conceptions of life and property were diametrically opposed to capitalist conceptions and intentions. Workers were treated as things and hired, not for their humanity, but only for their work energy. "Man is treated as a _thing_ to produce more things."[15] Workers were paid only enough to keep them alive and without regard to their need for human development. Christian faith would reverse the way industry was organized so that it would serve first the needs of the family and the individual. Economic science was written to support the going system and, by focusing on increased production rather than the problem of consumption, it had neglected human needs.

The social consciousness of Christianity, according to Rauschenbusch, radically qualified ownership rights. Owners hold all in trust as administrators and they are not free to exercise the power of property arbitrarily. He applauded President Theodore Roosevelt's attempts at regulation of corporations and trust busting, but he left open the possibility that, if such efforts failed, another group in the next decade would have to insist upon public control and oust the owners from control.

His socialism separated him from more liberal reformers of his day
and distinguished him from the progressives. He knew that the propertied
class controlled the politics and dominated the legal process for their own
ends. His hopes were that instruments for turning the ownership of capital-
producing machinery over to the working class could be found. The only permanent solution to the impoverishment of the working class would be that
class' ownership of its tools. He expected that elements of the professional
classes would join with the workers, but he expected little assistance from
the middle class. The economic crunch was the major motivation for the social
evolution to common ownership, and the major effort would have to come from
the class being hurt most. He supported the labor movement and trade unionism
in their contemporary conflicts, but he argued that only through a socialist
or communist resolution of the class conflict could the workingman regain his
independence, his tools, his dignity and the full proceeds of his work.
"Socialism is the ultimate and logical outcome of the labor movement."[16] He
saw that the movement was only "tinged with socialism as yet"; however, he
thought its development and the reaction against it would push it in the
socialist direction.

He expected strong reaction against his 1907 writing which articulated a radical restructuring of society. He argued for "A new type of
Christian manhood which seeks to overcome the evil in the present world, not
by withdrawing from the world, but by revolutionizing it."[17] This process
of revolutionizing the world was engaged in supporting social forces moving
toward communism.

> Christianity certainly has more affinity for cooperative
> and fraternal institutions than for competitive disunion.
> It should therefore strengthen the existing communistic
> institutions and aid the evolution of society from the
> present temporary stage of individualism to a higher form
> of communism.[18]

The identification of the church's present social task with the urging of communism drew less criticism than was anticipated, and probably because his book did not attack specific individuals or corporations. Andrew Carnegie and Theodore Roosevelt drew praise and, though insights of Marx and other socialist leaders leap from the pages, it was the more mild Christian socialism of Maurice or Kingsley that was praised.[19]   Though expecting the working class to push for the social change and some professionals to ally with the movement, the book was directed specifically and only to the churches. It was a book for persuading educated Christians, and its impact was greatest upon young Christian socialists like Norman Thomas and Reinhold Niebuhr.

In contrasting the book's concluding chapter, "What To Do," to Lenin's 1902 essay, "What Is To Be Done," the greater specificity of Lenin is clear. Lenin's writing here is much more engaged in the control of his party. He too studies the evolution of his institution, in his case the party of Russian Social-Democracy, he too criticizes its past mistakes, but he is serious about dominating it and insisting on its revolutionary task. Rauschenbusch shares Lenin's passion for the change of his respective country, but he lacks the passion for wielding an instrument for the change. Both men have hopes, idealistic hopes in 1902 and 1907 respectively, but Lenin had a technician's mastery of his institution. In Rauschenbusch, the history is much grander, there is a passion for the church becoming an instrument of social revolution, or at least assisting the working class in their upheaval, but there is not the same desperateness in insuring that the institution is shaped for the task. Of course, Lenin was in exile, while Rauschenbusch was a professor at home in his land. But beyond all their differences of temperament, personality, mind and vocation, this different attitude toward their institution is evident.

Social Christianity failed in the United States partially because its leaders did not institutionalize it successfully. They were so concerned to regenerate all human institutions that, in many cases, they became alienated from their own base, the church. Worshipping God, they relativized the church and neglected to control it. Social-Democracy failed in Russia partially because there was no way to criticize the iron-bound party that Lenin had honed to a sharp edge for the revolution. The dictatorship of the proletariat became the dictatorship of Stalin, and before he died Lenin knew much of his work was defeated. Of course, the very victory of Lenin in Russia in 1917 contributed to the Red Scare of 1920-1921 in the United States and to the dread of revolution which helped undercut the Social Gospel which, on the other hand, saw many of its programs co-opted by the New Deal of the 1930's.

Rauschenbusch's goals were socialist or communist and, in Christianity and the Social Crisis, he uses the terms interchangeably, but he did not have a program except for the conversion of the church to the social gospel. He was not, in the 1907 book, naively optimistic about accomplishing that end, nor was he simplistic about the chances for social regeneration as were many of his fellow participants in the movement. He wrote:

> In asking for faith in the possibility of a new social order, we ask for no Utopian delusions. We know well that there is not perfection for man in this life: there is only growth toward perfection.
>
> . . . .
>
> At best there is always but an approximation to a perfect social order. The Kingdom of God is always but coming. But every approximation to it is worth while.[20]

Certainly on a scale measuring optimism and pessimism, he is heavily on the optimist side, but he shields himself from the utopians. He longs for change; he believes the hidden God of history is involved in bringing it about. He sets himself to awakening the church to what is happening. Yet he does not immerse himself as thoroughly as did Lenin in the struggle for his respective institution. If his social renewal did not occur, within his thought it was finally because God was not yet ready to bring it about. To say that his program was less adequate than his hopes is a less severe indictment than to level the identical charge at a Lenin, within whose theory the manipulation of history by the tightly-organized, controlled party was central.

Rauschenbusch is the most adequate of the theologians of the American social gospel movement. He was overly sanguine about the state of the American Republic's health and too uncritical of its racism and imperialism. The ideals of communism and of democracy were probably subject to more erosion in history than he anticipated. He was optimistic, perhaps naively so, about the family, the church and the state. However, he kept his eye on economic issues and did not fall into illusions that capitalism would produce social justice. He was relatively realistic about the corrupting influences of militarism. He saw the need to transform Christian theology from an overly-personalistic base to a structural perspective. He tried to define both sin and salvation in social structural terms while holding to individual responsibility. His contribution is represented in part by the actual suffering that he prodded his readers to alleviate. The embodiment of the social gospel in the church, in chairs of applied Christianity in seminaries, in social action agencies in church structures, and in innumerable programs is in part due to his influence. His influence on a generation of young clergymen laid the basis for a social theology being picked up again in a different climate. In the mid-1930 despair over American life, a theology closer to the pessimistic side of our theoretical spectrum would articulate the passion for social justice learned at Rauschenbusch's feet in different tones. Two world wars and a cold war, nuclear weapons, population pressures, crises in black and white relations, the discovery of poverty, and pollution issues separate our time from that of Rauschenbusch at the turn of the century. However, the task of finding an adequate synthetic strategy for renewing our institutions and of funding that strategy with a hope which does not shatter in the face of reality into illusion and despair is still our vocation.

VI. THE DEVELOPMENT OF AMERICAN POLITICAL REALISM

The decline in religious enthusiasm in the 1920's caused foreign
missions to decline, ecumenical projects to be unfulfilled, the respect for
the clergy to wane, and the action projects of the social gospel movement to
stir less interest. The depression and the exposure of the emptiness of the
Versailles Treaty contributed to break the spirit of optimism which the social
gospel had shared with the culture. Two sons of the social gospel first
worked together in socialist causes in the early 1930's, but in the 1940's
Norman Thomas continued to develop socialism while Reinhold Niebuhr went in
another direction. The political realism discussed in this chapter was self-
consciously formulated by Reinhold Niebuhr and Hans Morgenthau as a corrective
to the American culture's easy optimism and over-reliance on rational solutions. Their political realism has very little in common with German theories
of political realism. It is very much an American social reforming school of
thought, but one directed against philosophical and religious tendencies
toward oversimplifying the hard problems of collective life. Political realism contains a theory of politics, but it is consciously a prescriptive movement, i.e., it urges certain forms of political behavior. The theoretical
observations of realism do not stray far from their polemical purpose of freeing U.S. foreign policy from idealism, particularly Wilsonian idealism. A
brief description of the outlines of the thought of one of the German power-
political theoreticians will, through contrast, illumine the discussion of
the origins of realism in the breakdown of the American social gospel. The
views of Morgenthau and Niebuhr are then expounded and the significant differences between them discussed.

Machtpolitik

Heinrich von Treitschke's lectures on politics at the University of
Berlin at the end of the last century represent a form of power politics
quite alien to the American realists. For Treitschke, humanity, fulfilled
only in the state, realizes itself in and through interstate war. War is not
barbarism but a holy ordeal willed by God, the outcome of which reflects
divine purposes. One is first of all a member of a particular nationality,
and only secondarily a member of the human race. The plurality of states is
an expression of human richness; no one state could fulfill the content of
culture. Sovereignty for Treitschke is confirmed in the right to recourse to
arms. Inasmuch as the essence of the state is power, the most powerful state
approximates the ideal state. War is the only thing which forces people to
forget their private provincial pursuits and identify completely with the
state. "War is politics" and people become a nation only through war. Judgment by arms is the evaluation the world puts upon the worth of a culture
and a people. The judgment is imperfect, of course, and often the temporary
eclipse of a state like Prussia under Napoleon obscures the judgment. Though
glorifying war and power politics, Treitschke does not subscribe to vulgar
Machiavellianism. Honest policies and honoring treaties are generally the
most profitable policies. Immoderate policies are to be avoided on grounds
of prudence. Though Christian virtues are irrelevant to the guiding of the
state, a sense of honor ought to be maintained. The counsels of prudence
which Treitschke enjoins are not altogether different from the counsels of
the American realists, but the basis of the counsels is different. Treitschke
advocated a form of power politics as a way of realizing the greatness of
German character. There are illusions of European and Germanic grandeur in
his thought which receive a metaphysical basis in a theory of power politics.

Treitschke exalts the sovereignty of the state and the rivalry of the nations

as a means of fulfilling an ideal for humanity. Raymond Aron has noted the

difference between the German Machtpolitik and American political realism.

> In crossing the Atlantic, in becoming power politics,
> Treitschke's Machtpolitik underwent a chiefly spiritual
> mutation. It became fact not value . . . . The German
> nationalists desired power politics for itself. The
> American realists believe they are obliged to acknowledge
> its existence and accept its law.[1]

A Protestant Ethic

Political realism as it evolved in the United States was partially a

movement to reform the Protestant social ethic. The social gospel had com-

bined sectarian and Calvinist motifs with a good deal of secular optimism to

advance Protestant ethics beyond individualism. The social gospel took insti-

tutions and economics seriously and called for their radical reform; but at

the same time it remained somewhat naively optimistic and largely pacifist.

The social gospel movement reached its zenith in the years immediately follow-

ing World War I in the celebration of the victories of Versailles and prohi-

bition and the expansive spirit of Protestantism. It was the articulate

minority within the mainstream of American Protestantism, but even at its

height it could not count a majority of the members of any Protestant church

within its ranks. It quickly collapsed and, by 1933, former followers of the

social gospel regarded it as dead. Many historical factors contributed to

its decline; Reinhold Niebuhr's polemics against its ideology are of particu-

lar interest here because they contained many of the ideas of political

realism.

Against its optimism about reforming institutions to express the

Kingdom of God, Niebuhr emphasized a dualism which consciously owed much to

Augustine and unconsciously was derivable from Luther. One could fulfill the

law of love in personal life but not in social life. Sin or prideful egoism
was exaggerated in the social arena to the point where the best that could
be hoped for was justice, understood as a tolerable balancing of the claims
and counterclaims of various groups. The Christian virtues were <u>directly</u>
relevant to personal life but were relevant to social life primarily as ideals
which, while impossible to fulfill, revealed the relativity of all social
achievements. Moral judgments in the political arena involved a heightened
degree of ambiguity because of the need to balance the competing claims of
groups which could not be expected to renounce their group interest. Whereas
the social gospel had attempted to realize directly the will of God in the
common life, the political realists regarded this as impossible because the
structure of the common life involved competition, rough justice, and coercion.

Over against a social gospel assumption that humanity was creating a
more moral social order, Niebuhr argued that: (1) there was no historical evidence for a doctrine of inevitable progress, (2) the Christian doctrine of
history was one of tragedy not inevitable progress, (3) the history of the
interwar period revealed little progress in international politics and the
Marxist analysis of the capitalist economic collapse was essentially correct.

Niebuhr stated the ethic of Jesus in more extreme terms than had the
social gospel. For him the ethic of Jesus was one of nonresistance, not one
of nonviolence. This analysis relegated the ethic of Jesus to a more transcendent position than it held in the social gospel, but it also cut the support from under those who were proposing nonviolence as the Christian ethic.
Niebuhr broke with the Fellowship of Reconciliation (FOR) over the use of violence by strikers. The majority of the FOR held to the position that strikers
ought not resort to violence, whereas Niebuhr sanctioned the discriminate use
of violence. He came to believe, for reasons of Marxist class analysis, that

nonviolent teaching would support the foes of reaction against the just demands
of the proletariat. Violence was wrong according to the ethic of Jesus, but
so was resistance. Justice, not the ethic of self-sacrificing love, was immediately relevant to the domestic struggle; and justice demanded the use of
violence. Niebuhr held out against sanctioning international war after his
Christian pacifism had been refuted by his analysis of Jesus' ethic and the
requirements of his analysis of the class structure. Once the ethical distinction between nonviolent coercion and violent coercion was blurred, the
outlines of the realist position sanctioning the use of discriminate force on
the international scene began to appear.

Niebuhr regarded much of the optimism of the interwar period of the
United States as due to oversimplified doctrines of humanity. He wanted to
emphasize both the grandeur and the misery of humanity and to insist that
both the extreme optimists and pessimists were wrong. Human freedom violated
doctrines of humanity which attempted to understand mankind in terms of either
rationality or nature. Both the social sciences and philosophy were necessary
to understand humanity, but they necessarily erred if they tried to comprehend
humanity solely in terms of either logic or nature. One was free to make
moral choices and to choose ultimate ends. Misery arose from the inevitable
choice of selfish egoism. The self promoted its own interest, heedless of the
interests of others, and thereby corrupted its understanding of itself and the
common life. For Niebuhr politics had to start with the desire to control and
balance common egoistic drives, not with schemes for the elimination of egoism.

Political realism grew out of this protest against the optimism of
both secular and religious forces in the post-World War I period, and it
attacked this optimism with an ethical dualism, a tragic view of history, an

antipacifist interpretation of a social ethic, and a doctrine of humanity
which insisted that insofar as politics was concerned the self had to be regarded as a sinner. In Niebuhr it was an attempt to find a Protestant ethic
adequate to deal with American social problems which were analyzed in Marxist
terms.

Hans J. Morgenthau did not take up political realism in an attempt to
reform the Protestant ethic, but he inherited much of Niebuhr's teaching. He
has repeatedly acknowledged his debt to Niebuhr, and his Scientific Man vs.
Power Politics reflects much of the argument of Niebuhr's Moral Man and
Immoral Society and The Nature and Destiny of Man. Morgenthau has joined with
Niebuhr in combating American political optimism as symbolized by the provi-
sion of the endowment for the Carnegie Center of International Peace that,
after the war problem had been solved, the funds were to be applied to the
resolution of other social problems. With their respectively Augustinian and
Hobbesian doctrines of humanity and their recognition of the essential anarchy
of international politics, they have repeatedly joined in attacking simplistic
schemes for the elimination of the struggle from international politics. They
also exerted a common critique of American politicians who obscure the nature
of the struggle through moralistic sloganeering. Woodrow Wilson and his war
to make the world safe for democracy is perhaps their favorite example of an
American politician conducting a moral crusade when he should have stayed
within the bounds of traditional diplomacy. Niebuhr particularly resented
Wilson's idealism because he personally joined in supporting a war which he
had previously regarded as foolhardy for a mixture of reasons, including
Wilsonian idealism and American nationalism. Morgenthau finds the capture of
morality by nationalism which characterized Wilson's policy continued in the
self-righteousness of American policy under John Foster Dulles, and in the

globalism of President Johnson's policy which assumed the role of an anti-communist crusade in the third world.

The above survey of the American character of the realist perspective has focused on the polemical sources of realist theory and suggested that American political realism has been shaped by its development as an opposition movement to certain characteristics of the American Protestant church, optimism, and moralism in foreign policy.

Hans J. Morgenthau

Within Morgenthau's system morality is regarded, as is the balance of power, as one of the limiting factors of national ambitions. The relationship of morality to international politics is threefold:

> First, morality limits the interests that power seeks and the means that power employs to that end. Certain ends cannot be pursued, and certain means cannot be employed in a given society within a certain period of history by virtue of the moral opprobrium that attaches to them. Second, morality puts the stamp of its approval upon certain ends and means which thereby not only become politically feasible but also acquire a positive moral value. These moral values, then, become an intrinsic element of the very interests that power seeks. Third, morality serves interests and power as their ideological justification.[2]

In the domestic sphere, morality influences power relations by fulfilling all three of the above functions. But in the field of international politics morality is used primarily as the ideological justification of power interests. The nation state, which is the final element in the field of international politics, has been able to proceed relatively unlimited by morality. Nations have equated the interests they seek with the claims of professed moral principles.

Morgenthau is aware that his own philosophy of international politics is built upon a particular world view. Particular doctrines of political science have their roots in assumed conceptions of morality, purposes, and

goals which it is not the task of political science to question. The particular world view and mores of a nation shape and limit that nation's foreign
policy.

The pursuit of power needs to be limited by the claims of ethics.
The Bible, ethics, and the constitutional structure of American democracy
have emphasized keeping the drive for power within limits. All the dominant
systems of Western ethics have recognized the universality of the drive to
power and have sought to limit it. The political systems and philosophies
which have exalted the struggle for power have become self-destructive,
Morgenthau claims.

There is abundant evidence witnessing to the relevance of morality
as a limiting factor of political means. The influence of moral principles
is most obvious to Morgenthau in peacetime when ethical inhibitions prevent
executions that would be politically expedient. Morgenthau regards the
decline in the once-common practice of assassinating military and political
leaders as indicative of moral influence. Bismarck, in contrast to Hitler,
though vicious enough in individual moves on the political chessboard,
honored and did not attempt to eliminate his opponent, France. Churchill
demonstrated the difference between a moral realist and an amoral one at
Teheran when he refused, in the name of British honor, to concede to Stalin's
plan to execute 50,000 German officers after the war. "The fact of the
matter is that nations recognize a moral obligation to refrain from the in-
fliction of death and suffering under certain conditions despite the possibility of justifying such conduct in the light of a 'higher purpose' such as
the national interest."[3] All the conventions and treaties regarding the conduct of war, though often violated, also bear witness to a growth of moral
reluctance to use unlimited violence as an instrument of foreign policy.

Only in the last half-century has the avoidance of war per se become an object of statecraft. No longer, Morgenthau argues, can the initiation of a war be declared a foreseen and directed culmination of a nation's foreign policy. War must now be interpreted as a natural catastrophe or as an evil act of the enemy. The propaganda campaigns to justify national actions and national protestations of innocence are indirect recognition of moral norms which nations often violate and sometimes completely overthrow.

Decline of Morality in International Politics

Morgenthau argues that the limiting force of morality has declined in international politics since the seventeenth century. As evidence of the decline he cites the failure of the world's decision-makers to acknowledge a common standard of values, the elimination of the old international society, total war, and the breakdown of traditional means of diplomacy. Viewing international morality as an effective restraint upon politics as impossible, he approvingly quotes Dean Roscoe Pound: "It might be maintained plausibly that a moral . . . order among states was nearer attainment in the middle of the eighteenth century than it is today."[4]

The most basic cause in the failure of morality to fulfill its rightful place in international relations is the disbelief of the people in objective standards of morality. Morgenthau bemoans modern humanity's loss of religiosity, i.e., a "dependence upon a will and a power which are beyond his understanding and control."[5] Humanity's loss of a sense of mystery, tragedy, and guilt has dehumanized it. In his "Reaction to the Van Doren Reaction," Morgenthau attacks the moral obtuseness of America and affirms his belief in moral truths which people do not create but find in the nature of the world.[6] He is profoundly aware of the skepticism which allows one to fulfill the cultic acts in the midst of one's unbelief. He writes, "Religion has become an organized social activity and the public demonstration of official piety, permeated with doubt and disbelief."[7]

The democratization of the conduct of international politics has also dealt a blow to international morality in Morgenthau's view. Reference to a rule of conduct presupposes an individual conscience which responds to the rule. When the conduct of foreign policy was definitely traceable to the monarch or his representative, these individuals could hold themselves morally accountable for the actions of their governments. Today the vast bureaucracy of foreign officers hold no common consensus as to moral requirements, and no individual conscience is responsible for governmental actions. It is one thing to say that George III of England and Louis XVI were subject to moral restraints in their dealings, and quite another to say that Great Britain or France today has moral obligations one to the other. Even the vast turnover in the upper echelons of the United States State Department reveals how nebulous any consensus of an international moral order is today.

Morgenthau's argument that no one can be singled out who is morally responsible for the conduct of foreign policy ignores a significant amount of evidence: DeGaulle dictated French policy; Johnson was constitutionally responsible; Eden resigned following the failure of his foreign policy. He is correct in his claim that there is no consistent interpretation in the United States as to the demands of morality in international relations, but there are individuals who are morally responsible for the conduct of United States foreign policy. Two cases in point are Eisenhower's assumption of responsibility for the U-2 incident and Kennedy's acceptance of the Bay of Pigs invasion as his mistake.

Morgenthau feels that the influence of morality upon international politics has decreased with the destruction of the old aristocratic set which

ran the political affairs of Europe in the seventeenth and eighteenth
centuries. The aristocrats shared family ties, a common style of life, the
French language, and common moral values with regard to how the political
game was to be played. The attempt of the Czar to hire Bismarck to work in
his foreign service is an example of the cordiality in international politics
of a past age. Though Morgenthau may overemphasize the graciousness of previous European politics, he makes his point that the contending powers of the
twentieth century are less limited by common values than their predecessors.

There are signs, however, of a developing moral consensus which
Morgenthau overlooks. The United Nations is serving to bring together diplomats and to create shared values, customs, and morals. Andrew Cordier has
pointed out how quickly the representatives of the new nations mature; he sees
one of the more important functions of the United Nations as training the
world's diplomats. Hammarskjöld emphasized the importance of "corridor diplomacy" which, through informal contacts, tended to form a community of diplomats. The decline in "supranational moral rules of conduct" may be at an
end, and the present trend may be toward a more universal recognition of
principles of international conduct as represented by the United Nations
Charter, UN resolutions, and the UN community of diplomats. The moral authority of UN resolutions varies with the degree of unanimity achieved in the
voting, with the methods used to achieve a majority vote, with the skill of
UN personnel in conducting their affairs, and with the degree of continuity
between the UN resolution and the traditions of approved international practice; but recognizing that particular resolutions have different degrees of
moral authority does not invalidate the assertion of common usage that such
resolutions have a moral authority.

Moral Confusion in International Politics

Modern nationalism has suppressed supranational ethics in the twentieth century, and the ability of the nation to exert compulsion upon individuals has increased. The nation has available vast means of persuasion due
to technological developments. The prestige of the nation has increased in
a time when loyalty to a nation may require the destruction of several thou-
sand lives by one individual in the name of national loyalty. The weight of
the national prestige and the decline of universal ethics combine to force
most people to bow to the orders of the nation.

Most people have sought to reconcile the tension between national
interest and supranational ethics by equating national mores with values that
should prevail over the world. The aura of invincibility that has surrounded
American political action and the universal claims of Marxism have tended to
polarize issues and to cause each of the superpowers to make unjustified
claims for its particular system. Claims of morality have been used to disguise the rivalry for power between the United States and the Soviet Union,
and there is a tendency to see the cold war in terms approximating the religious wars of the Crusades. The equation of universal ethics with national
goals inserts an element of fanaticism into the competition.

> The morality of the particular group, far from limiting
> the struggle for power on the international scene, gives
> that struggle a ferociousness and intensity not known to
> other ages. . . . Thus carrying their idols before them,
> the nationalistic masses of our time meet in the interna-
> tional arena, each group convinced that it executes the
> mandate of history, that it does for humanity what it
> seems to do for itself, and that it fulfills a sacred mission
> ordained by Providence however defined.
> Little do they know that they meet under an empty sky
> from which the gods have departed.[8]

Equating supranational ethics with national interest is not only
politically disastrous; it is also morally indefensible. The Greek tragedians

and biblical prophets stand against the pride that equates a particular
nationalism and the will of providence. The blasphemy of identifying the
will of God with national political interests is clearly illustrated by ministers serving one God blessing warriors and arms on opposite sides of the
battleline. Against such expressions of idolatry Morgenthau's polemics are
consistently directed.

Morgenthau makes plain in his In Defense of the National Interest
that one of the major problems of United States foreign policy has been the
creation of an artificial dichotomy between national interest and moral principles. The substitution of moral principles for national interest is both
an intellectual error and a perversion of morals. The national interest has
an inherent dignity. Only by each nation maintaining order and preserving
its national community can even minimal values be realized within each nation.
Politics presumes the existence of power and interests, and to separate a
nation from the pursuit of its interests is to violate the art of politics.
"The choice is not between moral principles and the national interest, devoid
of moral dignity, but between one set of moral principles divorced from political reality, and another set of moral principles derived from political
reality."[9]

As a philosopher of international politics, Morgenthau is concerned
that the method of policy formulation be as rational as possible. He believes
that the confusion of morality and the pursuit of national interest in the
minds of American policy-makers have weakened American foreign policy. He
admits, after his tirades against American moralism, that in spite of moralistic speeches the United States has usually tended to act, as all nations do,
in power-political terms.

Morgenthau believes that all human action is corrupt. He refuses to reconcile ethics and political action and avoids three traditional ways of obscuring their differences: the end-justifies-the-means doctrine, the justification of action by intention, and utilitarianism.

"The tendency to justify otherwise immoral actions by the ends they serve is universal. It is merely most conspicuous in politics."[10] His central attack upon the end-justifies-the-means doctrine is based upon subjectivity of the relationship itself. The relationship of ends and means is totally relative to the particular social vantage point of the observer, he argues. One person's means may be another person's ends. The question of which political group is to be sacrificed can never be decided objectively on the basis of this doctrine. No ethical distinction between various types of political action can be drawn on the basis of this doctrine, since all actions are judged in relationship to the intended goal. The very concept of end implies a termination of political action and reaction which never occurs. This end-justifies-the-means doctrine has been seen in its most brutal form recently in the communistic societies which have permitted great personal suffering for the absolute good of the arrival of communism. Since the end-justifies-the-means doctrine has no objective criterion of decision, it tends to reduce ethical judgment to the intention of the actor.

The criterion of good intention for the judgment of action is especially irrelevant to the field of international politics. The very social relevance of political action is obscured by judgment on the basis of good intention. The good-intentioned, politically naive actor may do more harm than the ill-intentioned, professional politician; judging their actions on the basis of good intention ignores the significance of their actions. Morgenthau quotes Abraham Lincoln repeatedly to stress the importance of results when judging political action.

> I do the very best I know how, the very best I can, and
> I mean to keep doing so until the end. If the end brings
> me out all right, what is said against me won't amount to
> anything. If the end brings me out wrong, ten angels swear-
> ing I was right would make no difference.[11]

The dominant school of ethics in the United States, Morgenthau

thinks, is utilitarianism, which teaches that acts are right inasmuch as

they promote human happiness. This school does not ask the ethical question

at all, Morgenthau maintains, but only tries to calculate rationally what

action will result in the greatest happiness. He dismisses this school rather

lightly by pointing out that even modern humanity cannot indefinitely remain

oblivious to the eternal ethical problems. Despite his critique of the utili-

tarian position it is difficult to distinguish Morgenthau's position from

pragmatism, the American version of utilitarianism. In foreign policy he is

a pragmatist quite close to Niebuhr; in another realm (he isolates for pur-

poses of analysis political man, religious man, moral man, etc.) he thinks

morality consists of principles found in nature. He is caught in a funda-

mental dualism with knowledge of a realm or moral principles which are inap-

plicable to foreign policy, the realm of his interest. He welcomes the means

of power politics, but feels guilty about so doing.

The View of Humanity and International Relations

Morgenthau's philosophy of international politics is based upon his

view of humanity. All political theory, according to Morgenthau, is grounded

in assumptions about human nature. The abolition of war, the primary problem

of civilization, is made infinitely complex because the numerous causes of

war have their roots in the conditions of the human soul.[12] He has repeatedly

asserted that the moral problems of international politics are but a peculiar

instance of the moral problems of every person's encounter with other people.

As power is a basic element in Morgenthau's political theory, so it is in his doctrine of humanity. In response to a question asking for a statement of this doctrine, he replied: "The lust for power is an intrinsic element of human nature. It is one of the basic innate tendencies of man. It tends to create societies. In various societies the lust for power may be viewed differently, or it may be differently channeled, but it is always present."[13]

The lust for power arises, for Morgenthau, out of the same source as the need for love, loneliness. Of all the creatures, only humanity is capable of loneliness. Humanity has a "need of not being alone," but in the end one cannot escape being alone. Humanity as a biological, rational, and spiritual being finds in its existential loneliness an insufficiency. This insufficiency drives one in search of love and power. Though a stable relationship of love implies a degree of power or the relationship would be nothing more than a "succession of precarious exaltations," love is basically the more satisfying and first-sought relationship. "Love is reunion through spontaneous mutuality; power seeks to create a union through unilateral imposition." In the final analysis, the power relationship is a frustrated love relationship; power seekers would rather be united in love. Morgenthau sees in the great political masters a demonic seeking for power which resembles the frantic compulsion of misguided lovers who, substituting sex for love, seek to find satisfaction by multiplying their sexual conquests.[14] The unity these people seek in love can never be obtained, and so they blunder through life toward their own destruction. Morgenthau acknowledges his debt to Tillich's insight that love and power are, at their source, united.

Morgenthau is deeply aware of the tragedy and sin of the human situation and does not hesitate to use the terms in his most sophisticated political writing. His view of humanity is represented by the following statement:

"Suspended between his spiritual destiny which he cannot fulfill and his animal nature in which he cannot remain, he is forever condemned to experience the contrast between the longings of his mind and his actual condition as his personal, eminently human tragedy."[15]

Humanity's fate has placed it in a world in which evil forces (not just the negation of good or the lack of education) ruin and destroy its best plans and highest dreams. Social problems are only rarely solved, but one must continue the battle realizing that even one's best efforts can produce more evil, Morgenthau insists. As evil is inevitable in politics, ethics in politics is the endeavor to choose the least evil action among several alternatives. The final tragedy is death, which every person faces alone. He believes that "our age has lost faith in individual immortality in another age."[16] The very response of one to death determines to a large degree how one will live life.

The lust for power in the soul of humanity creates the power drives in international politics. The quest for certainty in the midst of uncertainty of each person characterizes the dogmatism of political claims. The egoism of self taints all political action, and the moral yearnings force one to reject naked human egoism as normative. Insecurity, the basic problem of humanity, is summed up by Morgenthau as follows:

> Man is a political animal by nature; he is a scientist
> by chance or choice; he is a moralist because he is a man.
> Man is born to seek power, yet his actual condition makes
> him a slave to the power of others. Man is born a slave
> but everywhere he wants to be a master. Out of this dis-
> cord between man's desire and his actual condition arises
> the moral issue of power, that is, the problem of justify-
> ing and limiting the power which man has over man.[17]

The sources of the human problem are insecurity and the drive to overcome this insecurity; salvation lies in accepting one's insecurity and acting in the full knowledge of the limitations of one's action. "The

achievement of the wisdom by which insecurity is understood and sometimes
mastered is the fulfillment of human possibilities."[18]

The Contemporary Moralism

Morgenthau regards the post-World War II drift in American foreign
policy toward the position that the U. S. is inevitably involved in all
international conflicts as the most dangerous tendency in American statecraft.
He believes that U. S. overinvolvement in world politics is due in part to a
streak of moralism in American foreign policy makers. This moralism is expressed in a worldwide opposition to communism or leftist revolutionary movements. Because it has posited communism or leftist revolutionary movements
as an evil to be opposed, U. S. policy has neglected to calculate carefully
the interests of the United States in particular cases. Despite State Department denials, U. S. policy has been set to oppose leftist forces wherever they
challenge the status quo. A wise foreign policy would weigh carefully the
threat of each revolutionary situation to the U. S. security or well-being.
The moralistic foreign policy is spared such intricate calculations because,
assuming the evil of the political left and the U. S. obligation to oppose
evil, the U. S. reaction to particular communist or leftist threats to the
peace is reflexive rather than reflective. Both of the two extremes in U. S.
strategy, isolationism and globalism, reflect a moralistic approach to
foreign policy.

> The isolationist's moralism is naturally negative, absten-
> tionist, and domestically oriented; it seeks to protect the
> virtue of the United States from contamination by the power
> politics of evil nations. Wilsonian globalism endeavored
> to bring the virtue of American democracy to the rest of
> the world. Contemporary globalism tries to protect the
> virtue of the "free world" from contamination by Communism
> and to create a world order in which that virtue has a
> chance to flourish. The anti-Communist crusade has become
> both the moral principle of contemporary globalism and the
> rationale of our global foreign policy.[19]

Reinhold Niebuhr and Hans J. Morgenthau

Niebuhr and Morgenthau were the leading figures in the realist school, but other significant thinkers took up their central concerns. Morgenthau's classic Politics Among Nations became the central text in the debates over the theory of international politics. Niebuhr's Moral Man and Immoral Society continued as the classic statement of Protestant social theory in the realist vein. The two thinkers were very close to each other. On one occasion, when Niebuhr was pushed to delineate the differences between his position and Morgenthau's, he replied:

> I wouldn't say that the views of Morgenthau and myself are "somewhat different." We basically have common ideas with certain peripheral differences.[20]

The most significant difference between the two thinkers is in the area of the relationship of ethics to politics. Morgenthau's view of political reality remained more tragic than that of Niebuhr. Niebuhr, who had held to a tragic view of history at an earlier period, came to regard history as more nearly ironical than tragic. It contained possibilities of gain as well as loss, and its configurations were continually producing surprises to both pessimists and optimists. These differences inclined Morgenthau to use ethics as a principle of criticism of politics. Ethical standards revealed that politics could not be the proper place for the good Christian. Niebuhr, on the other hand, used ethics both as a source of criticism and as a motivation for action. Politics was just the place for the good Christian, who was a responsible sinner. Niebuhr criticized Morgenthau for his overly consistent pessimistic interpretation of life. He also was not as secure as Morgenthau in regarding the national interest as the bearer of value. Niebuhr would admit that empirically nations usually did attempt to pursue their own interests, but he countered that normative thinking could not be surrendered to

this practice. The essence of the morality of international politics was
finding ways to permit the reconciliation and adjudication of the various
national claims, not sanctioning the individual nation's pursuit of its interest. He addressed to Morgenthau the remark: "Nations as well as individuals
stand under the law: 'Whosoever seeketh to gain his life shall lose it.'"[21]
The comparison of Morgenthau and Niebuhr reveals a gradual move in both thinkers toward a more moderate realism.[22] This development led Niebuhr to question the use of national interest as a term carrying its own moral dignity,
and events of history led both men to criticize United States policy in Southeast Asia in moral as well as political terms.

Niebuhr and Morgenthau surprised many of their admirers by their
attacks upon the Johnson Administration's war in Vietnam.[23] Were not these
thinkers, along with George Kennan, et al., the proponents of containment,
cold war politics, and the use of power to counter aggression? The subtleties
of their positions were ignored by many who, seeking simple answers, wanted
global answers to particular crises, who did not understand how nuclear detente
changed international politics, who sought a crusade where the realists wanted
calculating, flexible, responsive use of the U. S. capacity to meet particular
crises.

Also, many realists, or at least those like Hubert H. Humphrey influenced by these men, continued to support the war policies long after all
justifiable excuses for supporting the American venture had been discredited.
Within the moral leadership of the church, those influenced by Niebuhr like
John C. Bennett, perhaps the most outspoken against the war, were opposed by
Paul Ramsey, who justified the major ingredients of U. S. policy under the
rubric of just war theory. On the major issue of foreign policy of the late
1960's and early 1970's, then, the realists divided. The divisions were deep

and reflected not only their different situations in life but differences in their ethical thinking and also in their judgments as to empirical reality.

The fissures among the realist thinkers were reflections, of course, of the deeper divisions within the society. The realist critics of the war found themselves often paired on speaking platforms or in demonstrations with long-standing critics of the United States government policy who were glad but also startled to find themselves linked with those whom earlier they had regarded as opponents. Defenders of the Administration, e.g., Paul Ramsey, sometimes expressed amazement that the followers of Niebuhr, whom he had counted on to be more moderate in the criticism of the wielders of power, were so morally outraged by the U. S. role in the struggle in Vietnam.

The effect of the Vietnam crisis upon the realists who opposed the war was to open their eyes wider than before to the dangers of militarism in the United States and to fresher appreciation of the fragility of democracy in the United States. They saw how easily national purposes and rhetoric were corrupted and how willing the establishment, academic, governmental and ecclesiastical, was to be corrupted. The conflict psychologically turned them from being defenders of the broad outlines of U. S. policy to the role of critics in exile from those who were making decisions in Washington, D. C. By providing an example of foreign policy which so flagrantly violated moral standards, it brought a new force into their moral critique of the United States. Rather than emphasizing the moral ambiguity of foreign policy, they proclaimed the moral horror of this particular policy. Realism as a practical philosophy was not intended by either Niebuhr or Morgenthau to contribute to the reification of certain concepts of international politics. The pair of thinkers both rejected as quite inappropriate to the sixties and seventies the earlier rhetoric and policies of the cold war. This shift is best represented in Morgenthau's <u>A</u> <u>New</u> <u>Foreign</u> <u>Policy</u> <u>for</u> <u>the</u> <u>United</u> <u>States</u>[24] and

in <u>Truth</u> <u>and</u> <u>Power:</u> <u>Essays</u> <u>of</u> <u>a</u> <u>Decade</u> <u>1960-1970</u> and in their mutual support

of Eugene McCarthy's quest of the presidency in 1968.

Niebuhr: The Kingdom of God

The Kingdom of God was clearly the master thought of the social

gospel movement of Niebuhr's youth. It is also a major theme of the new

theologies of hope and revolution. It is not the major motif of Reinhold

Niebuhr's theology, but it is present. Scholars[25] have often been aware of

the contrast between the schools on either side of Niebuhr's dominant influ-

ence in American social ethics with his own thought on the subject and have

treated his theory of ethics as if it were independent of the Kingdom.

Niebuhr's ethic was more in the prescriptive mood than the indicative.

That is, he emphasized duty, the commandment of love, principles of justice

rather than relying primarily on a sense of the Kingdom moving to development

in history. He took account of as many of the empirical conditions as he

could be informed upon, but he would not regard the shape of the Kingdom as

empirically present in history. He also avoided the use of the Kingdom con-

cept overly much because it had gotten so tarnished by sentimental Christians

who had expected either its catastrophic supernatural arrival and who became

socially irresponsible or who expected evolution to produce an Americanized

version of the Kingdom.

However, despite the above qualifications, the Kingdom functions in

his thought in an important way. The best discussion of his on the Kingdom

is found in the last two chapters of <u>The</u> <u>Nature</u> <u>and</u> <u>Destiny</u> <u>of</u> <u>Man</u>. Here he

clearly states: "We must seek to fashion our common life to conform more

nearly to the brotherhood of the Kingdom of God."[26] Such an assertion, if not contradicted in the remainder of his thought, is a clear indication of the continuity of the social gospel in this thought.

Finally, for Niebuhr, though, the relationship of Kingdom and history is one of paradox. "History moves towards the realization of the Kingdom but yet the judgment of God is upon every new realization."[27] History continues in its incompleteness always needing those who will act resolutely to help complete it, but also requiring that they be able to comprehend why their actions will not complete it. The Kingdom of God was a guard for Niebuhr against utopianism and, he thought, a protection against the cynicism that resulted from utopian failures.

Perhaps because he personally was not tempted by defeatism, he could emphasize the transcendence of the Kingdom rather than its historical realization. But, as in all profoundly Christian theologies, the symbols are all present and the differences among the social theologies become matters of emphasis.

The argument of this study is that more emphasis upon the immanence of the Kingdom, a sense that all history is carried forward by God, greater openness to revolution, and an emphasis upon the transforming, liberating quality of the Christian message are all desirable. The shift in the various chapters is subtle to some, perhaps, because all of these possibilities are there in Niebuhr's own thought. It is a matter of emphasis. The danger is that, unless Christian realism establishes itself as a perspective that can sustain the long task of transforming our present structures into structures of freedom adequate to human life, it will be blown away. There is no particular loss in the perspective being eclipsed unless it is replaced by perspectives of heedless optimism and political naivete. From the perspective argued for in this book, it is better for Christian social ethics in this country to remember fondly its foundations in both Rauschenbusch and Niebuhr

than to ignore either of them.

The chapters discussing revolution and counterrevolution will empha-

size contributions from Niebuhr such as the following:

> The new world must be built by resolute men who "when
> hope is dead will hope for faith"; who will neither seek
> premature escape from the guilt of history, nor yet call
> the evil, which taints all their achievements, good.[28]

. . . .

> Life in history must be recognized as filled with inde-
> terminate possibilities. There is no individual or interior
> spiritual situation, no cultural or scientific task, and no
> social or political problem in which men do not face new
> possibilities of the good and the obligation to realize
> them.[29]

. . . .

> There is no limit to either sanctification in individual
> life, or social perfection in collective life, or to the
> discovery of truth in cultural life; except of course the
> one limit, that there will be some corruption as well as
> deficiency of virtue and truth on the new level of achieve-
> ment.[30]

The emphases of the above quotations are from Niebuhr, but they do

not contradict Rauschenbusch. Rauschenbusch was a little heedless in his

optimism, as was his time; Niebuhr's time was a defensive one for the United

States. Political ethics will have to combine sobriety about the staggering

crises facing mankind and passion for justice to enlist the energies of the

people.

VII. A PERSPECTIVE ON INTERNATIONAL POLITICS

Philosophers and political scientists have attempted to construct general theories to explain the relations between nation-states. At the present time, the attempts to provide an adequate general theory to explain the political behavior of nation-states have failed. Many empirical studies have provided data upon which general theorizing could proceed. Institutional analyses have taught much about how the tools of foreign policy are utilized. Many excellent histories of foreign policy and of international politics provide conceptual overall views of the relevant past which could be used for the construction of general hypotheses of explanation. Case studies have given to the would-be theorist episodes examined in depth upon which he hopefully could generalize. All of the study, though, has not provided the discipline of international politics with paradigms or models of understanding which could produce a prevailing consensus among scholars in the field. The theorists have the building blocks of general theory, but they have not been able to put them together. Economics, which has major divisions within its ranks of scholars, is a relatively ordered discipline in contrast to the confusion that prevails among the students of international politics.

Typologies of International Relations Theory

Recognizing the undeveloped nature of the study of international politics, several theorists have sought ways to present typologies of the various explanations given for the conduct of international politics. A brief survey of the typologies of theory of Kenneth Waltz, William T. R. Fox, Stanley Hoffmann, John Stoessinger, and Kenneth Thompson reveals the divergency in the field but also some interesting convergence.

Kenneth Waltz[1] has posed to the tradition of political philosophy the question: What is the fundamental cause of war? He divides the responses from the Greeks to the contemporary social scientists in three categories. Some answer: The fundamental cause of war is in the tendency within human nature to engage in conflict. Others reply: The problem is in the nation-state itself; the evilness of the state produces wars. The third group finds the cause of war rooted in the anarchic structure of the international system. Waltz himself opts for a model which has room for all three answers. The character of the interstate system makes possible, as Rousseau saw, conflict between the nations. The character of the people and the quality of the states provide the particular forces which give rise to specific conflicts.

William T. R. Fox conceives of theory as the means by which various perceptions of international relations are evaluated. In his view, Christian realism would be one of many theories, and the task of the theorist is to identify and evaluate it.[2] At one level of the analysis of the "theories" of international relations, he ranks the theories on a continuum relevant to the role of human choice they consider operative in the making of foreign policy. The doctrinaire realists have relatively little place for human choice; the empirical realists give a small place to the role of choice on the part of the policy maker; the pragmatic meliorist sees policy primarily as choice among a wide range of alternative actions; and the utopian theorist posits almost unlimited power for the policy maker to choose his policy. Fox conceives of himself as a pragmatic meliorist, but his refusal to take the title of realist is primarily due to his wish to avoid what he regards as the extremes of those he would call doctrinaire realists. In any case, the relevant range of theoretical debate for Fox rests somewhere between pragmatic meliorism or moderate realism, to use the term of the preceding chapter.

At a second level of analysis, Fox distinguishes between three types
of theory. All of these three types would be options within the limitations
of empirical (moderate) realism or pragmatic meliorism. Some theorists
would emphasize the distinctive features of each country's foreign policy.
Other theorists give special attention to the general principles by which
all states seem to behave. A third school would focus on the key relations
between particular states. The first group would tend to explain the invasion
of Egypt by Britain, France and Israel in 1956 by reference to the particular
features of those nations, to their sense of national interest, destiny,
pride, and to the available sources of power to those countries. The second
would focus more on international agreements, the United Nations and general
principles of state behavior interpreted either realistically or idealisti-
cally. The third school would have placed greater stress on the relationships
of Israel to the Arab world, Britain to the Suez Canal, Britain and France to
the U. S., the NATO alliance, the Soviet Union to the area, the post-colonial
world to Europe, etc.

Stanley H. Hoffmann, like the theorists already mentioned, believes
that the field of international relations studies suffers from disorder. One
function of a theory of international relations is to say what international
relations is, and what factors are not to be included in the field. He thinks
that theory can be classified by reference to the purpose it is intended to
serve. The term theory can then be applied in three different ways: There is
normative theory, which studies politics in terms of desired goals, e.g.,
Kant's theory of securing the good of mankind and perpetual peace through
world federation; secondly, there is empirical theory, which seeks to understand causal relationships, analyzes political behavior and identifies major

variables in the conduct of international relations, e.g., Hobson's theory
of the influence of capitalism and imperialism; finally, there is the policy
theory, which is intended to be advice on how to conduct foreign affairs,
e.g., Machiavelli's theory on how a prince should conduct his policy to get
and keep his throne. Hoffmann rests his hopes in the discipline on progress
in the realm of empirical theory, but he recognizes the need for the other
two types and asks mainly that the distinctions between the three be honored.[3]

Kenneth Thompson[4] has pointed to an agreement among several scholars
at a conference in 1955 to agree to utilize for the conference discussion
Walter Lippmann's typology for the theory of international relations.
Lippmann proposed the distinctions between normative theory, general theory,
and theory as the basis for action. Lippmann's categories, upon which
Hoffmann's seem to depend, did not produce agreement as to exactly what
should be done within each type of theory. Lippmann's claim that there are
rational sequences and causal relationships which can be generalized upon
serves the needs of Hoffmann for a general empirical theory and avoids the
problems that the term empirical suggests. These distinctions seem to indicate different motifs of various theories, even if actual theoretical works
appear to mix elements from all three types.

Another way to look at the field of international relations theories
would be to divide it in four ways, as John Stoessinger has done.[5] He
regards Hans Morgenthau and his followers and fellow critics as composing
a group that could be roughly labeled "the power school." The term quanti-
fiers could be given in a general way to a disparate group of theorists who
are trying to build the theory of international relations upon models imported from other fields. The systems theory of Morton Kaplan, the communica-
tions theory of Karl Deutsch, the decision-making theory of Richard Snyder,

and the game theory of Jessie Bernard are representatives of this group.
The case study technique is a mode of operation of many of the outstanding
theorists of international relations. In much of his work Professor W. T. R.
Fox exhibits the power of the case study approach. Another school of increasing importance is composed of those who draw upon psychology for their
insights into international relations. The best known work of this type is
probably Harold Lasswell's World Politics and Personal Insecurity.

The school of thought under consideration here as Christian realism
does not fit any of the types of international relations theory suggested.
Aspects of it may count as part of the respective theories, but it would seem
that Christian realism is not a theory of international relations, but a perspective on the political relations between nations. It is a perspective in
the sense of a practical philosophy which contains a philosophy of life,
ideas about how nations relate, normative theory, and a history of many policy
recommendations. The most adequate way to show what this perspective means is
to put it in the context of the difference between an idealist and a realist
approach to international relations.

Idealism vs. Realism

Christian realism is a perspective on international relations which
partakes of the policy-oriented characteristics that Hoffmann, Thompson and
Stoessinger noted. It is interested in providing policy advice to statesmen
and to the public which it thinks influences policy. It makes use of empirical or general understandings of international relations inasmuch as they
help the formulation of appropriate policy. It has a large component of
normative theory in its perspective. The normative aspects of what ought to
be are always in tension, however, with what is. Christian realism as it

relates to American foreign policy is the attempt to promote certain long-range foreign policy goals of peace, order, and justice while taking account from both theological and political perspectives of the forces which resist those goals.

Realists have for decades carried on a polemic against those they considered guilty of too casually trying to replace diplomacy with a grand design for world order. Plans like some of the proposals for turning the United Nations into a world government have evoked their wrath.[6] Other plans of world safety or rapid total disarmament schemes have often seemed apolitical to the realists, who refuse to urge statesmen to surrender their responsibilities for nation-states. The schemes to displace the rather awkward system of politics with a perfect government have reappeared from Dante to Kant to the present. This tradition of idealism emerged with a vengeance after World War I and the establishment of the League of Nations. The idealists have been able to present their plans over against known failures of the interstate political system. The realists have countered with questions like: Are the grand designers willing to go to war to force their system on a reluctant world? Would not a world government drift toward tyranny in the absence of world community? Is it responsible to ask a statesman to scrap his institutions on the hope that an idealistic system will work better?

Against those who would replace diplomacy as the art of international politics with various grand plans, the realists have insisted upon the political aspects of the major problems. Cooperation among scientists does not result in nuclear disarmament. Consultation among the leadership of various religious groups does not produce brotherhood. Feeding populations does not eliminate war. The education of people does not produce agression-free statesmen. Goodwill trips and cultural exchanges do not deeply affect the

passions and emotions of the masses of nations. In short, the realists see
international politics as a realm of intensive struggle and some cooperation.
The Christian realists understand these dual drives, toward national power
seeking and international community building, as having their roots in the
nature of humanity and its history.

The realists' quarrel is with what they regard as a too-easy moralism
in the United States. Americans tend to be unsophisticated in assuming the
rightness of their cause, the goodness of their motivations, and the appropriateness of claiming moral sanction for national policy.

Though the realists disagree among themselves on many important
issues, it is possible to speak of them as a school of thought. Kenneth W.
Thompson[7] has isolated five elements that are common to the individuals discussed here as a school of thought: (1) They tend to avoid moral absolutes.
Though the movement has part of its origins within the struggle to reform
Protestant ethics, it has become deeply involved in planning and recommending policy. (2) They reject attempts to escape from the problems of power
politics. International politics is the search for national security in a
very frightening context. (3) They have deep distrust of theories of moral
progress or utopian plans. They tend to assume that, though the present
system is risky, for the relevant future the mutual interplay of independent
nation-states will continue to be the context for international relations.
(4) They exhibit a passion for the study and interpretation of history.
Stanley Hoffmann, following Raymond Aron in _Paix et Guerre entre les Nations_,
calls for a historical sociology of international politics. Pages of Hans
J. Morgenthau's _Politics Among Nations_ and Reinhold Niebuhr's _The Structure
of Nations and Empires_ provide examples of such reflection. (5) They agree
that a rather explicit doctrine of humanity is helpful to political thought.

As noted above, they do not hold themselves to one doctrine in the school.
There is a predominant tendency, however, mostly due to Niebuhr's influence,
to take very seriously the Augustinian understanding of humanity expressed
differently in Luther, Calvin, Hobbes, Montesquieu and Madison, and to avoid
highly optimistic pictures of the race.

Critique of Realism

Raymond Aron, a leading French theoretician, has accused the realists
of mixing theory and the science of policy making (praxeology). He feels
that their failure to distinguish adequately between perennial and contingent
features of the international scene leads to confusion. This criticism is
true in part; they do tend to judge theoretical insights by practical results,
and they explain practice in terms of broad theoretical considerations. They
are, in part, political essayists with a philosophical bent. Walter Lippmann,
their major journalist, publishes works on social philosophy, while their
major theologian writes hundreds of journalistic articles on politics. When
they were close to power in 1947 on the Policy Planning Staff Committee of
the State Department under George Kennan, they worked explicitly on the
development of a body of theory which was applicable to United States foreign
policy. Aron is correct that they move quickly from reflections on theory to
judgments on the quagmire of foreign policy. The movement, of course, is not
one of deducing practice from theory; rather it is a practical judgment util-
izing theory and empirical data. Whether such movement is as ill-advised as
Aron seems to think remains an unresolved issue.

Stanley H. Hoffmann has subjected the realist school to a thorough
critique.[8] The organization of his attack is rather loose, making it difficult to outline his major points, but there seem to be six general points.

1. Realist theory fails because it views the world as static, in
which the relations between nations endlessly repeat themselves. He thinks
this is true because the realist understanding of power is too limited. At
various points he charges that Morgenthau's understanding of power is (a) confined too closely to a limited set of variables, (b) too nearly equated with
violence and evil, (c) portrayed as an end whereas it should be seen as merely
an instrumental concept. Hoffmann makes his point that _power_ as used by
Morgenthau has more ambiguity than should be tolerated in a key concept.[9]
This ambiguity, or even improper use of _power_, hardly freezes the realist
theory into a static world view. The realist theory of Morgenthau and
Niebuhr, rather, seems to engage itself with questions as to how power relations among states are to be understood in a new nuclear age. Both theorists worry about the impact of ideology and revolution on the conduct of
foreign policy. Niebuhr's book on imperialism is a study in how the phenomenon of one nation controlling others has changed in different empires and
epochs. The charge of articulating a philosophy in which "power relations
reproduce themselves in timeless monotony"[10] would be a severe one if it were
not so far removed from their actual work. Hoffmann's general point that more
rigorous analysis of key concepts (e.g., national interest) is needed is a
fundamental challenge to the realists to sharpen their distinctions.

2. Hoffmann's implication that the realists treat international
politics apart from reflection on national politics and processes is not true.
Hans J. Morgenthau's _A New Foreign Policy for the United States_, Reinhold
Niebuhr's _The Irony of American History_, and John C. Bennett's _Foreign Policy
in Christian Perspective_ all treat foreign policy as a reflection of domestic
politics, fears, national history and public ideologies. All three participate in internal national debate for the sake of influencing international
relations.

3. The suggestion that sometimes the realists have assumed national interest to be too clearly defined is a reasonable critique. Hans J. Morgenthau's early In Defense of the National Interest made this mistake. John C. Bennett's rather careful analysis of the national interest in Foreign Policy in Christian Perspective or Morgenthau's polemical articles criticizing administration understandings of the national interest belie the suggestion that this is an essential weakness of realist theory.

4. Hoffmann criticizes the realists for asserting that morality in international relations is determined by national interest. The preceding chapter showed that Niebuhr would not treat national interest as the determiner of morality. Morgenthau's point is that national interest, properly understood, carries a certain moral dignity as it bears the hopes, interests and security of a people. Most realists use the national interest as a corrective against idealists who would engage in crusades for various causes. The realists want to limit policy to what can be defended as promoting a prudently defined national interest. Morals cannot be deduced from national interest; if some of Morgenthau's statements imply it could be, he was mistaken. Morgenthau's more customary position, though, is to see morality as one of the factors that limits nations from pursuing their interests through power.

5. Hoffmann misunderstands realist theory when he criticizes it for overreliance on the "rationality of foreign policy." Realist theory assumes one to be anxious and passionate in politics as one is in sexual life. Politics is not a science, but an art. Still the responsibility of the theorist is to be as rational as possible in explaining the irrationality of politics. If Hoffmann had taken more seriously the realist theory of human nature contained in Reinhold Niebuhr's Moral Man and Immoral Society and Hans J.

Morgenthau's <u>Scientific Man vs. Power Politics</u>, he would not have raised

this point of criticism. Rather than regarding the political process as

rational, they often criticize other approaches to international politics as

being overrationalistic. Hans Morgenthau leveled precisely this critique at

Richard Neustadt's institutional analysis approach.

> Professor Neustadt's abortive attempt to overcome the
> hazards of foreign policy with knowledge is the latest but
> probably not the last undertaking of this kind. . . .
> Academics in particular are forever searching for the
> philsopher's stone that will show them how our rational
> propensities can be superimposed on a rationally intract-
> able reality. They have not succeeded and cannot succeed
> because they are up against the immutable nature of foreign
> policy which yields to intuitive hunches about someone's
> actions and perceptive estimates of changing historical
> forces but not to prediction derived from complete knowledge.[11]

Whether or not he is overly hard on Neustadt's study, his criticism is cer-

tainly not the critique of a rationalist.

6. The final point of criticism, that realist theory does not

seriously attend to those activities taken by extragovernmental forces in

international relations,[12] reveals Hoffmann's own desire to set international

relations as a master paradigm for the other social sciences. Realists,

though, having interests and writing extensively (perhaps too prodigiously)

on most human endeavors, try to limit the study of international politics to

a set of relationships which can be studied. All of life, e.g., the relation-

ship of humanity to nature, religious loyalties, ideological conflicts, are

considered in the theory but only as they affect the quest for power, peace,

or security on the international scene.

Hoffmann's critique, in summary, reveals that the realists are in

need of more rigorous analytical work in some of their concepts, but his

attack fails to deplace the realist model from its central role in understand-

ing international relations. Much of Hoffmann's explicit attack was limited to Morgenthau's thought and probably to only some of Morgenthau's writing.

Another valuable type of critique was that undertaken by a panel[13] of theologians who focused explicitly on Reinhold Niebuhr's understanding of Christian realism. Underlying the discussion was the general feeling that a philosophy articulated in the 1930's, 1940's and 1950's would have to be revised for the late 1960's and 1970's. All of the panel members knew that Christian realism was flexible and could adjust to changing situations, and so they undertook to discuss how it should evolve. John C. Bennett, the one in the panel closest to Reinhold Niebuhr by the longest association with him, indicated that the phenomena of the nature of nuclear war, changes in the Communist world, the need of revolutionary change in much of the world, and the peril of American counterrevolutionary tendencies were forcing adjustments away from the earlier cold-war stance of Christian realism.

All the panelists agreed on the desperate straits of the American republic in the late 1960's. Many of them found the philosophy of Christian realism unable to suggest ways to deal with revolution, technology, and the imaginative life styles of the counter-culture. Occasionally they suggested that Christian realism had a conservative prejudice, but they knew that the charge was irrelevant to the philosophers they were discussing. It was more that the mood of Christian realism was prudent action, while the mood of the times and many of the panelists was revolutionary rhetoric. While realism asked the professors to imagine they were calculating statesmen, some of the professors wanted to imagine they were revolutionary leaders.

Many of the theologians, especially Shaull, Cox and Driver, exhibited uneasiness over the lack of imagination in Christian realism. They called for a revival of apocalyptic motifs and the legitimization of utopian thought. Others were very suspicious of the usefulness of apocalypticism to politics.

Though the panel could not agree on a proper formula, it appeared that there was a consensus that hope deserved a larger place in Christian theology than it had recently received. Hope that is not illusion can stimulate wise action and help desperate people continue the search for possible avenues of social change.

Though uneasiness about Christian realism had prompted the reevaluation, the discussion indicated that it had not yet been deplaced in political ethics. With a few minor exceptions, the uneasiness could not be translated into alternative paradigms of understanding political reality in theological perspective.

The evaluation of the critique of realism has to this point suggested that, generally speaking, the realists were wiser than their critics. The criticism often rested on a misreading of the realists or upon rather exotic notions of politics resting on the quicksand of the latest fads of the counter-culture. There are certain points of critique of the realist school as it has influenced U. S. foreign policy that must be made.

1. The realist analysis tended to separate too widely the demands of conscience and the realities of politics. There was no need for their polemics separating moral reflection from political reflection. They polemicized against the moralism of Woodrow Wilson, John Foster Dulles, et al., with statements that were too broad for their targets. They argued against the influence of morality in foreign policy when their real opponent was a misconceived understanding of the relationship of morality to politics.

2. They helped cripple political liberalism with statements that dismissed the whole liberal tradition. In fact, they were and remained liberals in political philosophy. However, the optimism and even sentimentalism of some liberals drove them to discredit the whole movement. Reinhold

Niebuhr particularly used liberalism as a synonym for optimism and sentimentality in politics.

3. They often failed to analyze central concepts rigorously enough. The terms power, balance of power, imperialism, all required more thorough analysis than they received at the hands of the leading realist philosophers.

4. As they achieved their greatest influence in the 1940's, 1950's and 1960's, they were subject to the weaknesses of their time. They shared in the dominant cold-war ideology of the American nation. Many of their works supported an overly dogmatic attitude toward Communism. They theorized as to how the cold-war competition should be continued, but they provided us with very little insight concerning the ending of the cold-war era. They did not spend much time developing the role U. S. initiatives could play in breaking the patterns of conflict.

5. They persuaded the churches and helped to persuade the country that world government was neither feasible nor desirable. They won their point that a tolerable world government would have to presuppose a tolerable world community. More suggestions about the first and second steps toward the achievement of a tolerable world community would have been helpful. Polemics against the illusions of many world government advocates are not enough; strategies for reducing nationalism and encouraging whatever internationalism is possible are needed. The realists have a hard-won credibility; assistance in helping conceptualize how to maximize multinational programs and international cooperation is required.

VIII. POWER AND PURPOSE

Contemporary American life reveals a disparity between purpose and power. The country claims to be powerful but it is unsure of its purpose. The Christian church understands the purpose of human existence but seems powerless in the face of social crises. The problem is both a practical issue and a failure to understand the relationship of power to purpose. The relationship between the two is a perennial question in social ethics. Each generation works at the problem, striving to resolve it fittingly for its time. No generation works at the problem in a vacuum; each thinker stands on the shoulders of those who have gone before and ignores their solutions at peril. However, the contemporary thinker cannot be bound by the solutions of the past, for his social context is different. Any attempt to appropriate the solutions of the past requires an interpretation of history which is only a contemporary understanding of that history. Therefore, though the solutions of our history are relevant to the contemporary relationship between purpose and power, they are not determinative.

Power and Purpose Divided

It has been the recent fashion to distinguish sharply between ethics and politics. In advocates of Realpolitik, the distinction has become a division. Polarities have been created between descriptive and prescriptive statements, between ethics and politics, between love and justice, and between purpose and power. The thesis of this chapter is that because the gap between purpose and power has been exaggerated by the "Neo-Machiavellians," a new understanding of the relationship of purpose to power is needed. Hoping

143

to purify morality, the "Neo-Machiavellians" artificially confined it to irrelevance. They campaigned for an autonomous realm of politics, but they robbed it of meaning. They portrayed politics as the war of every person against every other person and international politics as the war of every state against every other state. The description of politics as a self-interested war is neither an accurate nor a helpful model. The division between ethics and politics stems from both an inadequate analysis of politics and an idealistic ethic. The supposed conflict between purpose and power resulted from a confusion about the nature of power and the irrelevance of certain dreams to immediate political issues.

The Ambiguity of Politics

There is an essential moral ambiguity, though at different levels, to both domestic politics and international politics. The society requires peace, order, and justice; but the society also requires the fulfillment of the vitalities of its respective parts. The state is simultaneously the desired prize of the various parties of the society and the instrument which preserves order and justice. The Utopians have seen the peace-keeping function of the state and have neglected the vitalities of parties of the society. The Machiavellians have pointed to the struggle for control of the state in preserving order and justice. The Utopians either lose sight of the vitalities of life or dream of mastering them through a legal system. The Machiavellians, often in reaction to the illusions of the Utopians, see nothing but the struggle and the prize of the state and regard law and ethics as ideological illusion justifying and reenforcing the position of those temporarily in power.

More and Machiavelli may be regarded as symbols of two different views of the state. The one regards the state as the agent of justice. The other

basically regards justice as irrelevant and views the state as the prize to
the victor. What divides them is the dualistic character of politics. An
adequate solution to the problem of the relationship of purpose and power
must take into account this dualism and recognize that, though More and
Machiavelli are powerful symbols of political life, they each basically represent only one side of it. It is necessary to recognize that throughout
history those who control the instruments of deciding and implementing justice
will exact a disproportionate reward for their distribution of justice. However such a view, whether based upon an Augustinian view of man or upon
generalizations from empirical observation, does not necessarily drive one to
the conclusion that justice is totally fraudulent or should be dispensed with
lightly. The modern welfare state reveals this moral ambiguity well. The
state is responsible for the fulfillment of a broad range of programs to promote the well-being of the population; however, the competition for the control of the state is conducted with very little regard for the welfare of the
people.

If the "realists" have not fully appreciated the dualistic character
of political life, neither have they understood ethics. One source of the
origin of the contemporary political realist movement was a protest against
certain tendencies of liberal Christianity. To reform the ethic of liberal
Christianity it was necessary to show that the teachings of Jesus were not
directly relevant to the reform of the industrial-military complex. The distinctive feature of realism was its tendency to emphasize the factors in
humanity's collective life which resisted moral solutions or pressures. Such
a corrective was needed; liberal American Christianity had been naive about
the relevance of Jesus' ethic to politics. In the case of some spokesmen of
the realist camp, however, the polemics against the too-easy moralization of

politics developed into the separation of moral considerations from the struggle for power. The attempt to correct heresy in the liberal camp became
heresy itself by overemphasizing its essentially correct insight, that man's
social life resists moralization.

Ethics is the critical inquiry into moral principles and the
quest for wisdom concerning the good life. Ethics then includes the search
for wisdom, temperance, justice, and courage as well as faith, hope, and love.
It inevitably involves considerations of one as a social animal. Humanity may
have religious concerns in its solitariness, but ethics involves one as a
social being. Strictly speaking there is no such thing as a personal ethic,
and realist attempts to divorce personal ethics from social ethics have not
been successful. They could not be successful because personhood inevitably
involves one as a social animal and, except in a mythical realm of nature, as
a political animal.

Power Reconsidered

The concept of power has played a central role in recent writings on
political theory. It has been the pivotal concept in realist writings. Hans
J. Morgenthau's volume, Politics Among Nations, bears the subtitle, "The
Struggle for Power and Peace," and most commentators see that volume focusing
on the struggle for power. Inis L. Claude's work, Power and International
Relations, finds Morgenthau's discussion inadequate, but still regards the
concept as the key to understanding international politics. Raymond Aron,
writing in a different political environment and a different sociological
theoretical tradition, shares the above theorists' fascination with the
inquiry after the meaning and analysis of power.

Claude devotes almost ninety pages to demonstrating that Morgenthau
and others use the term equivocally. Probably Morgenthau's use of the word

can be deciphered in each particular context, but all of the furor over
Morgenthau's understanding of the concept points to a real problem. Morgenthau risked lack of clarity in his concept of power by deliberately using it
very broadly. He argued:

> The value of any concept used in political science is
> determined by its ability to explain a maximum of the
> phenomena that are conventionally considered to belong
> to a certain sphere of political activity.[1]

His criteria of breadth produced ambiguity. His further elaboration that "By
political power we refer to the mutual relations of control among the holders
of public authority and between the latter and the people at large,"[2] left the
term too general for the purposes he wanted to make of it. It also implied
something that Morgenthau himself would deny, that those "mutual relations of
control" are measurable without calculation of the goals, situation, and peculiar features of the actors involved. The implication that the struggle was
over means, i.e., "mutual relations of control," and not ends was almost inescapable even though that was not Morgenthau's intention.

Niebuhr's use of the term varied from essay to essay and alternatively made use of three major meanings. There was _power_ conceived as the
vitality of life or energy, which was neutral as regards value choices. It
was a given. There was the _power_ which was one person's or society's hegemony over another, which was a result of the sin of pride. The moral connotations of control were essentially negative as control was rooted in a person's prideful response to his anxious condition. The third use of _power_ had
positive connotations, as it was the expression of social organization. The
cohesiveness of the social organisms produced a power which, in turn, helped
to further the unifying process within the society. The three uses of power,
with value connotations of neutral, negative and positive, made it difficult
always to understand what Niebuhr intended by his use of the term _power_.

In the most general sense, power means the capacity to do, to make
or to destroy. Paul Tillich, who in our generation has demonstrated the
greatest capacity for becoming articulate about the general, defines power
as being overcoming nonbeing. Power is the self-realizing capacity of all
that is. He expresses his general definition of the term, "Power is the possibility of self-affirmation in spite of internal and external negation."[3]
This definition is particularly apt when the power of a nation which is
threatened both from within and without is under consideration. An understanding of power in international relations ought not to stray too far from
this general understanding of the concept.

Theories of international relations often list the elements of
national power even when the theorists are not clear about the meaning of
power itself. H. J. Morgenthau lists: (1) geography, (2) natural resources,
(3) industrial capacity, (4) state of military preparedness, (5) population,
(6) national character, (7) morale, (8) diplomatic skills. N. J. Spykman
focuses on the following elements: (1) surface of the territory, (2) nature
of the frontiers, (3) size of population, (4) raw materials, (5) economic
and technological developments, (6) financial system, (7) ethnic homogeneity,
(8) degree of social integration, (9) political stability, (10) national
morale. Guido Fischer listed essentially the same factors under the headings
of political factors, psychological factors and economic factors.[4] These and
other lists resemble each other, but in themselves they do not provide adequate theory; they only point to factors to keep in mind when estimating a
nation's power.

The enumeration of such factors is useful and causes problems only if
it is taken too seriously. Such lists do not provide relative weights to the
various factors, nor do they show how the weight of each factor varies from

situation to situation. The listing of such factors is a disservice only if
statesmen mistake such lists for science. F. C. German's essay, "A Tentative
Evaluation of World Power,"[5] which actually assigns numerical values of
various factors of area, population, gross product, military personnel, stra-
tegic air power, planned economy, represents the absurdity of thinking that
power can be measured abstractly without reference to goals or situations.
His results were not too surprising; perhaps his ranking of countries according to their power represented the reigning common judgment of American political scientists. North Vietnam did not even make his list of almost a score
of "powerful" countries. The problem of such thinking is that it does not
adequately protect the insight that politics depends upon contingency and
passion. Clausewitz, who in many ways was very rationalistic, still knew
that, "War is the province of chance." Barbara Tuchmann's history of the
beginning of World War I, The Guns of August, is a powerful antidote against
the illusion that international politics can be rationalized or even that the
role of movement of armies and men can be planned accurately in war.

The approximate calculation of a nation's capacity to make war in
certain prescribed ways, if many variables are assumed to be known, is possible. In our present world, when the ways of war, either nuclear or guerilla,
are unknown even to the best strategists, great humility about the calculation of power is in order. Probably the attempt to compute power, except
with a full consideration of particular situations, should be abandoned and
our rhetoric changed to account for the new realities.

The quest for an understanding of ethics and politics which will
respect the dualistic nature of politics while avoiding the errors of Utopianism or Machiavellianism requires a reconsideration of power. Can power be
conceived in relationship to purpose? Can it be conceptualized in any other

way? Vietnam provided the primary example of the difficulty of speaking of

power in static terms. If military force were power, the United States had

overwhelming power in Vietnam but could not realize its purposes. Was it

helpful to speak of the United States as a "superpower" and Vietnam as a

"power vacuum" if the United States could not prevent its allies from engag-

ing in religious persecution or even guarantee the freedom of its own press

there? By all the conventional indices of power--population, military

machine, morale, efficient organization, economic base, etc.--the United

States is a very powerful nation. However, many reports from Vietnam indi-

cated that the United States was powerless to persuade its allies to reform,

its enemies to surrender, or the population to adopt its cause. The conven-

tional use of the term power to mean a static entity belonging to a nation

forces a paradoxical description of the United States as both powerful and

powerless. Paradoxical language is sometimes justified, but in this case it

reflects confusion in the usage of the concept of power.

The confusion which inevitably results from defining power in such

static terms as force, money, position in hierarchy, etc., is eliminated by

conceiving of power in relational and purposive terms. A definition of

power[6] which eliminates the confusion of the static approaches and also recon-

ciles power with purpose is the following: power is the capacity to produce

intended effects (purposes) in relation to others (field of action) under

certain conditions (context or understanding of the context). The power of

an actor depends on his goals, the domain in which his action is intended,

and the context in which his action is to be executed as well as upon his

ability to draw upon the sources of power--be they geographic, military,

organizational, traditional, economic, or ideological. Applying this under-

standing to Vietnam, it can be seen that the United States had power to

fulfill certain purposes but lacked the power to fulfill others. It follows
that delineating the purposes of policy was a prerequisite of any estimate
of United States power in Vietnam. It also follows that the debate about
United States objectives in Vietnam was more relevant to a Vietnam solution
than controversies about stopping the bombing, the timing of negotiations, or
legitimizing the military junta that governed Saigon. The emphasis upon purpose in an understanding of power indicates the relevance of moral considerations to power politics, for one who would deny that the selection of goals
is free from moral considerations and ethical reflection has misunderstood
the meaning of ethics.

Christian Purpose and Power

The mainstream of Christian thought has consistently held that political power is of God. Government as an order is instituted by God through
sinful men to act as a limit upon their sinfulness and as a source of order
and justice for their lives. Love and power are regarded as ultimately united
in God and eschatologically united in the fulfillment of history in the
Kingdom of God. Within the broad confines of the tenets of Christian attitude toward political power, there have been endless variations on the relationship of political power to Christian purpose. Five motifs of the relationship of purpose and power stand out in bold relief from the maze of intricacies
characterizing the Christian purpose. These five motifs do not represent a
typology of Christian response to power, for the word types implies mutually
exclusive systems. Motifs suggests distinguishable characteristics which can
be used complementarily.[7]

The first motif is that of the opposition of Christian purpose to
political power. Christian purposes are defined in terms of radical love and
a hope for renewed life. Political power is suspect because it is connected

with a dying, passing world. The Christian lives a fundamentally apolitical
life because the Kingdom of God is not of this world. Whenever the kingdoms
of this world are judged by the standards of Christianity, they are found to
be profoundly lacking in harmony, justice, and charity. Tertullian exposed
the contradictions between the Christian purpose and political power by emphasizing the degree to which political power depended upon military force.
Christian purpose was antithetical to political power; and the use of military force for Christ had, "in disarming Peter, unbelted every soldier." The
motif of the opposition of Christian purpose and political power was predominant in the young church, but it is reawakened in each age of Western history
when some theologian or sect takes with utmost seriousness the radicalness of
the love ethic and emphasizes the brutal nature of political power.

At the opposite pole is the motif which harmonizes Christian purpose
and political power. This harmonizing is characterized by the selection of
certain movements in political life as representative of Christian purpose.
It may be expressed in very traditional states; for example, the divine-right-
of-kings doctrine as it was elaborated for the rise of the absolute nation-
states harmonized the requirements of Christ and the needs of legitimizing a
relatively stable but parochial manner of assuring the succession to the seat
of government. On the other hand, when Christian revolutionaries proclaim
Christ as a revolutionary they represent the harmonizing of Christian purpose
and one type of power. The harmonizing of Christian purpose and power in
traditional, liberal, or radical ideologies has the advantage of releasing
the energy of absolute devotion for what are considered valid political
causes, but it has the disadvantage of obscuring the moral ambiguity of the
political order.

The previously considered motifs represent extremes within the church's thought on the relationship of power to purpose. H. Richard Niebuhr has delineated three middle positions in his typology of Christian ethics: the synthesists, the dualists, and the conversionists. Transposing his categories to the discussion of the relationship of purpose and power allows them to be expressed as: purpose regulating power; purpose and power understood dualistically; and purpose transforming power.

The ideal of Christian purposes regulating the institutional life of man in a direct fashion was expressed by Thomas Aquinas at the end of a period in which the church was gradually winning control over a Europe recovering from the destruction of the Roman Empire. In theory, Christian ideals were supreme, and in fact the church was supreme in many instances. The church accepted responsibility for all of society. The church accepted the wisdom and the institutions of the world while regarding its own wisdom and institution as higher. It attempted to Christianize the culture it accepted without identifying itself completely with that culture. In terms of power politics, when the church was consistent with this motif, it insisted that public policy serve its purposes.

Augustine provided a dualistic answer to the question of the relationship of purpose to power. The world was characterized by two communities. Both communities sought peace which, when fully understood, included justice. Both communities were subject to God's purposes and derived from God's power. In this world the two were intermingled. God's purposes and power for the two cities differed. The City of Earth founded in the love of self was given power to limit chaos and to preserve, through coercion, a type of peace. The City of God, founded in the love of God, gave people the peace of God which included salvation and true justice. The Christian was a citizen of the City of God and a sojourner in the City of Earth, and he was enjoined not to love the passing things of the City of Earth. The Christian may work through politics; but when he does he must utilize the means of power, even though they are in themselves corrupt. The ways of earthly power were symbolized by Babylon, and though a Christian might use them they were not to be loved. "Let us sit by the waters, not beneath the waters, of Babylon. . . . Sit by the waters, not in the waters, not under the waters." Augustine's writing includes several of the suggested motifs of purpose and power, but its most representative view is that of the state having both purpose and power from God but in a different manner from the church's purpose and power.

The motif of Christian purpose transforming political power was predominant in the social gospel of the center. To the degree that Walter Rauschenbusch maintained that the Kingdom of God was not to be realized by men and that structural change was required to complete man's salvation, he represented this motif. The moderates of the social gospel advocated a mild form of socialism while judging all means to achieve socialism by Christian principles of morality. They hoped for an immanent renewal of society through the political process. The democratic process was at hand, and they hoped to realize Christian ends by working through the process. It was fundamentally a reform movement; many of its advocates, particularly Rauschenbusch, recognized the degree to which human selfishness was stifling the fulfillment of Christian life. Social gospelers disagreed regarding how much reform was necessary for the regeneration of the social order, but they agreed that their faith was relevant to the utilization of power to rebuild American society.

There is a movement in Christian ethical scholarship to refuse to exclude polemically any of the major motifs of Christian ethics from consideration.[8] All of the five motifs discussed have strengths and, in certain contexts, definite weaknesses. The relationship of Christian purpose to political power cannot be decided abstractly but will depend to a significant extent upon the form of the institutionalization of the political process as well as upon the shape of the purpose. The Christian who excludes from consideration any of the above motifs cuts himself off from a possible source of Christian wisdom. Relating the best combination of the above motifs to particular political situations depends upon the habit of prudence.

Though the question considered here cannot be solved for all time, a contemporary resolution of the relationship between Christian purpose and political power is required. Within the pluralistic societies of the West where Christians are free to advance their purposes through the political process, the most appropriate motif is that of purpose transforming power, corrected by the emphasis upon the dualistic nature of the relationship of purpose and power. This motif which has evolved on democratic ground needs to be modified by an Augustinian realism about the frustrations of political life. It is also the motif that is consistent with an understanding of power as the fulfillment of particular purposes in relationship to other selves under specific circumstances.

National Purpose and Foreign Policy

Christian purposes are not the same as the purposes of a nation-state, though considerable overlap may exist. The argument of the preceding pages assumed that in some sense purpose or the definition of goals would be an ingredient of power. Christian goals focus on the liberation of people to develop to their fullest capacity as worshipers of God and responsible participants in society. National purposes are pushed by the Christian to take on the shaping of life so that man is liberated to develop fully. Probably nations should remain vague about their ultimate allegiances while permitting

and encouraging citizens to seek adequate definitions of their ultimate loyalties. Nations do not need to include the proper worship of God in their
understandings of purpose while citizens inevitably must define their ultimate
convictions in religious or pseudo-religious terms.

Nations must continually seek to understand their purposes in the light
of shifting circumstances and the conscious development of their peoples. The
purposes of the nation will condition, to a large degree, the way the resources
of the country are used to affect the future.

The realist tradition has hidden the concept of national purpose within
their own concept of national interest. In their writings on the morality of
international politics they have attempted to show how the pursuit and/or
defense of the national interest is a moral policy. John C. Bennett reveals
his own sensitivity about pursuing the national interest but accepts the inevitability of conceiving international politics in terms of the national
interest:

> Whenever we think about the moral issue involved in
> the behavior of nations, we must come to terms with two
> major concepts, the concept of national interest and the
> concept of national power. I shall discuss these in turn.
> It would perhaps be easier to teach Christian ethics in
> a world in which neither existed, but that is not my privi-
> lege.[9]

National interest, contrary to the quote, does not exist. It is a concept.
It may be a helpful idea or a poor idea, but an idea it certainly is. It is
possible to conceive of international politics without the difficult concept
of national interest. The difficulty of national interest rests in the ambiguity of the term. It carries connotations of a concept around which debate
can arise. Under this use of the term, the concept is value laden and consists basically of what the policy-making elite decide is the national interest.
The government of Great Britain agrees to the dismemberment of Czechoslovakia

and months later goes to war over the invasion of Poland, and both are in the
national interest as it is conceived by the policy-makers at the different
times. The other meaning of national interest stresses the more "objective"
side of the phrase. A strong economy, a favorable balance of trade, strong
military defenses, secure borders, etc., are said to be in the national interest. Debate can go on as to how much oil needs to be imported, or how much
of the scarce mineral resources of the world need to be controlled, but seeking and controlling resources is part of the national interest. It is this
second use, particularly, in which national interest is taken to be self-
evident that confuses the discussion of international relations. National
interest too easily becomes a slogan which stops the political process. Debate
is cut off because the national interest is being pursued. People who debate
over national policy in terms of national interest find it very hard to suggest
that fundamental shifts in policy must be affected. The economic thinking of
the government presses toward the conclusion that, if the U. S. economy needs
roughly 35 per cent of the raw materials of the world to function, it is in
the national interest to secure access to those raw materials. Prior questions (e.g., whether or not the purposes of Americans are served by that
economy and that scramble for resources) have no way to enter into the debate
on equal terms with the economic needs, once the whole question of policy is
perceived in terms of national interest. Sensitive people do not construct
their models of life solely on their own interests. They articulate models
of social existence and conduct in terms of fitting responses in a world in
which many beings coexist. Their actions take on a goal orientation; they
articulate their actions growing out of needs in terms of purposes which are
compatible with the articulated purposes of other selves. So with nations,
they do not pursue interest, at least not in the second sense of self-evident

quantifiable interests, but they pursue rather sophisticated purposes which contain their needs, their dreams, their morals and, of course, their illusions and their pride.

The above analysis suggests that American policy is not intelligible on the basis of understanding any quantifiable definition of the national interest. It further implies that the ambiguity of national interest renders it particularly inappropriate for a discussion of foreign policy. Purpose is a more helpful concept than interest. Purpose is rooted in the national history of a people and the definition of purpose is a function of poet and philosopher as well as the lawyer turned statesman. Definitions of purpose will vary; foreign policy varies. Our foreign policy is the temporary synthesis of American self-understanding as translated through the foreign policy apparatus in its attempt to realize the goals of some Americans beyond the borders of the nation.

The Christian statesman for our time and place is the one who knows that a grasp of Christian purposes is relevant to the struggle for power. Though the struggle for power is strange to Christian purpose, the greatest power comes from the appropriate merging of goal and means. Purpose and power are united finally in the political actor, or he falls prey to cynicism or impotence. It is this merging of the purpose of Christianity with the means available that is the strange and awesome work of one who attempts to embody Christian statesmanship.

IX. REVOLUTION: CONCEPTUAL ANALYSIS AND NORMS

There is no immediate prospect of the United States becoming a revolutionary power. The country has, since 1917, repeatedly been an antirevolution-
ary nation. Our recent experience in Vietnam, in which we failed to demonstrate the impossibility of wars of national liberation, may free us to
substitute a more critical perspective on revolutions for our semi-automatic
actions of opposition to revolutionary movements. The conviction of "no more
Vietnams" could conceivably force the United States into an isolationistic
defensive policy. Such a policy, though ultimately dangerous to the U. S.,
would be better for the world than our current anti-revolutionary stance.
Reflection on American ideals and interests, however, makes this isolationistic policy seem unlikely. The real range of policy debate seems to lie
between our present anti-revolutionary phobia and a policy of critical examination of particular revolutions. The cry of "no more Vietnams" may free us
to look more carefully at revolutionary movements and to raise new questions
concerning the revolutions which will occur in many countries in Asia, Latin
America, and Africa. Vietnam has discredited the automatic "no revolution is
tolerable" position, and Americans who desire a rational foreign policy are
forced to think again about the meaning and norms of revolution in our day.
This chapter undertakes the limited but important task of clarifying the meaning of revolution and of thinking ethically about responses to revolutions.
It does not evaluate particular revolutions or suggest which revolutions
American citizens should support. Rather, it suggests ways of thinking about
the concept revolution and the norms for response to revolutions. The essay
presupposes that the most important thinking about revolution is to be

159

undertaken at a level roughly equidistant from the current anti-revolutionary
stance of U. S. foreign policy and the romanticism of uncritical support of
revolution per se.

The argument of the book so far has established that the gospel of
the Kingdom of God has, in many situations, undercut the principles of
legitimacy upon which regimes based their authority. It has been claimed
that throughout The Old Testament and The New Testament the downfall of many
orders and the critique of others has met with God's favor. The church has
been revolutionary, not only in its sectarian forms, but also in its more
establishment institutional forms. On the other hand, the church has also
been used to buttress established regimes, including more and less just
orders. Marxian revolutionary theory has emphasized the church as part of
the anti-humanist ruling establishment. The critique of Marxism's own inade-
quacies does not refute the insight that the church has often supported
retrogressive forces. Realist theory has encouraged resistance to communist
tyranny in the name of insights grounded in Christian perspective. The
resistance of realism often unintentionally complemented radical anti-communist
movements in the United States which were fed by religious presuppositions
quite different than those of the Christian realists.[1] The climate of the
cold war, American self-interest in the status quo, a certain imperial self-
righteousness, anti-communism, and particular perceptions of security interests led the nation into its counterrevolutionary stance. The argument of
this chapter is intended to show ways of critical moral thinking beyond cold
war stereotypes or romantic revolutionary rhetoric. The setting of such a
discussion imposes limits on the meaning assigned to revolution. The attempt
here is to sort out, of all the broad meanings of the term, a political definition which will permit some precision in the normative inquiry which follows.

The meaning of the concept _revolution_ is illusive. Borrowed from
astronomy, the term came to have its current uses in eighteenth-century
France preceding the crises and wars of 1789-1794. Its use has been expanded
from its meaning in politics to apply to fundamental changes in philosophy,
religion, economics, patterns of industrial organization, and social organization. The meaning of the term sought here is one which will root its meaning centrally in the politics of a given society and distinguish it adequately
from other concepts like political evolution, coup d'etat, civil war, war of
independence, etc. The meaning of the term should not stray too far from
the common usage of the concept, but it should be possible to refine the concept sufficiently to order our political discourse.

The highest degree of precision possible at this level of generality
ought to be our goal. Since it is presupposed that ethical reflection on
revolution is desirable, the definition given to the term should not be so
laden with prescriptive elements that our attitudes to the phenomena we call
revolutions are predetermined by our labeling process. In other words,
formally it must be possible to distinguish between desirable and undesirable
revolutions.

A survey of contemporary writers on revolution reveals many different
definitions, and furnishes a basis in the usage of the term by political
philosophers for further refinement. Craine Brinton isolates as the core
meaning of the term the drastic sudden substitution by violence or subterfuge
of one ruling group by another.[2] Carl J. Friedrich defines political revolution "as a sudden and violent overthrow of an established political order."[3]
C. B. Macpherson is concerned to distinguish _revolution_ from coup d'etat or
"palace revolution." He means by revolution, the use of unauthorized force
to transfer political power for the aim of occasioning fundamental change in

social institutions.[4] Hannah Arendt stresses two factors in her discussion

of revolution: novelty and freedom. The goal of a revolution is the new con-

stitutional establishment of freedom.[5] Eugene Kamenka is concerned to dis-

tinguish between rebellion and revolution. The rebel is seeking to redress

grievances, while the revolutionary has a goal of a new order and progress.[6]

He confines the term revolution to convulsive changes to avoid regarding

history as one continuous revolution. He suggests as a preliminary defini-

tion the following:

> A sharp, sudden change in the social location of political
> power, expressing itself in the radical transformation of
> the process of government, of the official foundations of
> sovereignty or legitimacy, and of the conception of the
> social order.[7]

Paul Schrecker defines revolution as essentially an illegal change in the

fundamental laws of a nation. His analysis emphasizes that this fundamental

shift in thought which is illegal by the standards being abrogated is paral-

lel to movements regarded as revolutionary in other areas of human life.[8]

The survey of the essentials of a definition of revolution provide an ade-

quate sample from the usage of the term in contemporary political philosophy

to permit the isolation of several factors in a definition of the concept

revolution. Of course, not all the authorities surveyed included the same

factors. The number of factors included depend upon the criteria chosen for

the defining process. This defining process considers the level at which

the process of change occurs, the nature of the change, and the group forcing

the change.

Political-social systems reflect different levels of support. There

is the broadest level of the entire social matrix, the narrowest level of the

particular government in power, and the intermediate level of the constitu-

tional structure within a given society. Coup d'etat and rebellion refer to

changes in particular governments and revolution to constitutional changes.
Revolution is more than a shift in the social forces; it is a reflection of
this shift in the constitutional structure of that society. This means that
it is preferable to stipulate that revolution involves a change in the constitution or the rule-making processes of a society and not just in the replacement of rulers.

However, there are many changes in constitution or regime. Some
changes are provided for within the constitution. These changes will not be
considered revolutionary because of a distinction that is necessary on the
level of the nature of the change. Common usage demands that the change be
an illegal rather than a legal change. In other words, revolution occurs when
there is a change in the constitution of that society which is illegal by the
terms of that constitution. The change in the canons of the rules of legality
is a defining aspect of the term revolution. The question of violence or nonviolence is not vital to the definition for though there may never have been
nonviolent revolutions, there is nothing in principle which makes the consideration of such change impossible.

The third factor to consider is the group involved in the revolution.
If the revolution changes the fundamental notions of how rules for a society
are to be fashioned, it seems natural to think of the revolution as that of
the dispossessed, discriminated-against classes. But such need not be the
case; an illegal regime change could take place under the leadership of the
privileged classes because of fears they have regarding their security,
ideology, or interests.

A distinction between illegal regime changes accomplished by domestic
forces and those carried out primarily by foreigners is needed. The important
discrimination to note here is the one between revolution and war. A

revolution, then, is any illegal constitutional change which does not involve another political system as a major factor. An illegal constitutional change resulting from foreign imposition is regarded as a result of occupation or dictation and differs radically from revolution. The distinction between intra-system illegal regime changes and inter-system illegal regime changes, which occur frequently, is needed.

Also necessary as a factor in the definition of revolution is the number of people involved in the process of effecting the change. Such a distinction is recognized in common parlance in the difference between popular and palace revolutions.

Another factor which could be considered in stipulating a definition of revolution would be the duration of the process. How long a period can a revolution occupy? Were there several French revolutions or one from 1789-1794? This factor does not seem vital to the definition, as the actual struggle to effect an illegal regime change within a given political system is usually meaningfully limited by salient conflicts.

In a diagram, this definition of revolution would appear as follows.[9]

The stipulative definition of revolution for this study is an illegal change in the constitution of a given political system by those governed by the laws of that system.

Discussion of norms for social life presupposes that they can be stated as general propositions which can be supported from many of the different traditions in the society. However, the motivations for choosing to attempt to live a moral life in society vary, and the statement of various norms will reflect particular traditions. The tradition of social ethics presupposed in this essay is that which regards social ethics as an interdisciplinary endeavor in which the insights of our religious traditions are related dialectically to the tradition of social philosophy. Political ethics for a religious community is the endeavor to formulate moral principles out of the critical reflection upon the theological traditions and political philosophical traditions which are part of our history. The principles are evaluated by criterion of utility in furthering the development of humanity. The meaning of humanity is never finally settled, but it is discussed in terms derived from the doctrine of man on the one hand and social science and social philosophy on the other.

A greater precision and clarity can be obtained in the area of social ethics than is always available in the execution of social policy. Such a gap is inevitable. Regarding revolutions, Edmund Burke is correct: "Time and occasions and provocations will teach their own lessons."[10] To recognize the fatefulness of the contingencies of history, however, is not to surrender social ethics; it is rather to recognize the humble place of social ethics while insisting that, because we want to be moral people, we must be as precise as possible regarding our moral judgments.

The context for the moral thinking which follows is that of American decision about future unnamed revolutions in the developing world. The prescriptions assume that Americans should not initiate revolutions abroad. Our understanding is too weak and the level of violence is too great to permit Christians of the U. S. to challenge order abroad for the sake of a new order. In American political theory, the final sanction for the authority of the government is that it governs with the consent of the citizens. This in

itself implies a limit on intervention in the affairs of other states. Originally U. S. democratic fervor was not universalistic in the sense of trying
to subvert regimes so that those countries could become democratic; rather it
was hoped that the example of an orderly republic would be an attraction for
various peoples themselves to attempt to follow the model of the United
States. The technology, economics and, to a lesser extent, the ideology of
the United States do have a transforming effect upon the world. There is,
however, a difference of great magnitude between recognizing the "revolutionary" effect of the U. S. on the world and sanctioning U. S. initiation of
political revolution abroad. Christians and others who think of political
matters as matters of conscience will often deplore suppressive measures of
other regimes, but the strongest moral objection to a regime is qualitatively
distinct from presupposing the wisdom and the power to cause a revolution in
another country. Americans, because of who they are, dare not dictate to the
third world the governments they should have or should overthrow.

Once a revolution has begun, Americans will find themselves involved
in terms of economic interests, ideological issues, security interests perhaps, personal ties with both the government and the revolutionaries, church
issues and interests, and concern for human welfare. The government of the
United States will be involved, probably supporting the status quo, and its
security and economic interests. The following guidelines are taken as principles by which we can evaluate a revolution which has begun and can decide
whether we will support the revolution, and the position we will urge upon
our government vis-à-vis the revolution.

The tradition of moral reasoning represented here is in continuity
with the major tradition of church moral thinking since the fourth century.
It affirms that love must be responsible and that responsible love involves

the protection of people even when the means used to protect those people are themselves awkward and even violent. The tradition presupposes the ultimate goal of Christian living to be the Kingdom of God and, in this history, the penultimate goals to be life in continuity with the structure of the Kingdom. As the Kingdom is an order of justice, cooperation and peace, characteristics like inequity, competition and violence are in tension with the Kingdom. Christian political ethics is the task of trying to act for the Kingdom with loving acts in the midst of a violent history. However, the Christian knows that his goal is a nonviolent order and that he stands in a tradition reaching past the fourth century to a nonviolent disturber of order named Jesus. So, when a Christian regretfully acknowledges that sometimes violence may be justified in the sense that it is the responsible action of love to be violent for the sake of people, he knows that such a choice is made with a searching of conscience. Violence will have no place in the Kingdom, and it is not loving to the one who is the object of it, and so it can only be used morally in very difficult situations. This is to affirm that the Christian reasons from a position close to pacifism to the regretful sanctioning of violence. One ought not to reason from a disposition toward easily accepting violence to justify particular actions. The tradition of just war thinking has been grossly misused; such misuse is inevitable. The tradition cannot furnish conclusions, but only general moral guidelines which we can use as the basis for further detailed reflection.

Just war thinking, in this case thinking about just revolutions, means that many wars or revolutions examined will be found to be unjust. That is no reflection on the adequacy or inadequacy of the moral theory. Christian ethics presupposes that unjust acts of various kinds are the normal fare of mankind in this age. Only occasionally will cases be found in which a

revolution is so clearly the correct act that Christians ought to support it.
Those cases do exist, and when they are known the Christian is restrained by
prudence but not by moral imperative from self-involvement, urging the church
to participate in helping the revolutionaries, exercising political pressure
so that the United States will encourage the revolution, and asking U. S.
business firms to assist the revolution.

Christians are sometimes obligated to act violently to overthrow
unjust structures of meaning and power. The growth of humanity has been
characterized by victories over structures which were retrogressive, but
which had to be overthrown since they did not collapse from their own decay.
James Cone and Jürgen Moltmann have both rejected the absolute contrast between nonviolence and violence as illusory. In too many situations dominating
the world, only violence or acquiescence in the violence of others, often
tyrants, is possible. Cone calls the question of violence, following Jose
Bonino, a "subordinate and relative question."[11] The question is rightly
subordinate for Christians who have worked it through their minds to that
point; for millions, however, who are only beginning to think in revolutionary terms, the question is a primary obstacle. Moltmann reminds the Christian
revolutionaries: "Only with great restraint can revolutionaries enter the dia-
bolical circle of violence and counterviolence if they are ever to conquer
and abolish it as a whole."[12]

The five principles stated here are in continuity with the tradition
of Christian ethics concerning just war and with the liberal-democratic tradition of the right of revolution. They are stated in terms considered relevant to the 1970's and, if elements of the above-mentioned traditions seemed
to have been outdated, they have been dropped from this contemporary statement.

1. A revolution should not be undertaken lightly, and Americans
should rally behind revolutions only when there are sufficient signs that the
order being overturned is intolerable to large segments of that order's popu-
lation. When the government has become so burdensome that it fails to fulfill
the purposes for which it was instituted, it should be overturned. John Locke,
following medieval patterns, spoke of an appeal to heaven when the government
was oppressing the people. For, when the government violates the purposes
for which consent to it is given, it no longer deserves the support of the
people. By appeal to heaven was meant, of course, an appeal to arms. In
Romans 13, Paul articulated what can be interpreted as a very conservative
attitude toward the order of government. He justified his position in part
with a utilitarian argument: "For government, a terror to crime, has no
terrors for good behavior." John Knox, a revolutionary Calvinist, seized on
this justification by Paul and asserted that, when a government _is_ a terror
to good behavior and has no terror for crime, it has no divine sanction.
Edmund Burke, whose sympathies led him to support the American Revolution
but to oppose the French, put the case in these words:

> Governments must be abused and deranged indeed, before it
> [revolution] can be thought of, and the prospect of the
> future must be as bad as the experience of the past. When
> things are in that lamentable condition, the nature of the
> disease is to indicate the remedy to those whom nature has
> qualified to administer in extremities this critical,
> ambiguous bitter potion to a distempered state.[13]

The state must be intolerable, and the best sign of the gross failure
of the state to fulfill its mandate is the suffering and opposition of many
of its people. Two regimes of recent history which have revealed this high
degree of failure are the obvious examples of Diem's and Batista's governments.

2. The revolution must have a good chance of success before support
is given to it. Some might argue that the government of the Dominican
Republic is intolerable, but there are no real possibilities of revolution
there. To support a revolutionary movement there would condemn many to death
and probably encourage a tightening of the already burdensome features of
Dominican life. The severity of life during the revolutionary/counterrevolu-
tionary struggle is too harsh to be encouraged lightly. One must be relatively sure that the preconditions for a successful revolution exist before
encouraging the revolutionary blows to fall. The world of revolution is a
violent, severe world with little romance, grace or humor, and we must be as
wise as serpents on entering therein.

3. The justification of support by Americans of a foreign revolution
also depends upon that revolution advancing humanity. Revolutions as defined
in this chapter can be retrogressive as well as progressive. They can be
undertaken to secure the special privilege of a minority as well as to open
society to a rising underprivileged class.

Revolutions from the landed aristocracy of Latin America are not
unlikely, as governments there try to haul their recalcitrant countries into
the twentieth century. Europe has seen fascist revolutions in this century.
Revolutions which are admittedly antiliberal or antisocialist in structure
are retrogressive. They are products of the nineteenth-century mentality.
Humanity's future forms of social organization are not clear but, if they are
to be progressive, they will include some mixture of socialist and liberal
virtues in their constitutions. Revolutions against these desired goals of
liberalism and socialism are not furthering humanity's advance.

4. The revolution ought not to involve a major risk of international
war. A liberal-progressive revolution in North Korea with a program for

greater justice engaged in by many of the Koreans should not be supported by
Americans because of the risk of war with China. Order with a hope of evolution is preferable in certain sensitive border states to a revolution with a
high risk of international war. Most revolutionary situations today do not
involve the risk of international war except by the action of the U. S. as a
counterrevolutionary power. As difficult as such calculations may be, U. S.
citizens should not neglect in their moral reasoning the response of the U. S.
to the revolution in question. "Many Vietnams" may be in the immediate interests of certain radical movements in the third world; they are not in the
interests of the U. S. nor in the long-range interest of the world community.

   5. *A final norm for the evaluation of a revolution is its relationship to violence*. Revolutions will probably require violence, probably a considerable amount of violence. The violence can be justified when the previous
order is so unjust as to be intolerable and when other means of change seem
unlikely to succeed. However, the acceptance of violence does not mean that
there are no limits. The case against violence in Christian ethics is almost
persuasive. But in this violent world the resort to violence to secure peace,
to reduce violence, to protect the innocent is accepted as a regretful necessity and drives us to live by forgiveness. However some revolutionaries,
through utopian fantasies, self-righteousness and tragic suffering become
inured to violence; when the leaders of a revolutionary movement accept unlimited violence as a policy, their movement hardly deserves the support of Christians for whom violence is a regretful alternative.

   Self-righteousness and failure of political imagination combined with
counterrevolutionary pressures to produce the terror of the French Revolution.
Robespierre justified his policy: "Terror is nothing other than justice,
prompt, severe, inflexible; it is therefore an emanation of virtue . . . it

is a consequence of the general principles of democracy applied to our
country's most urgent needs."[14] The terror, of course, consumed the revolutionaries themselves and heralded the end of the bright, bold experiment in
a dictatorship.

A revolutionary party which refuses to limit violence or to protect
civilians and which engages in a systematic general policy of terror does not
deserve the support of the Christian conscience, no matter how unjust the
regime and how ideal the announced goals of the party. Means as well as ends
need to be evaluated. Part of the fruits of a party like Robespierre's is
the suffering of the innocent, and by such fruits we have to judge them.

All of the above is to say that there is a prejudice in Christian
ethics in favor of avoiding violence and, in these extreme cases of revolution, of limiting it.[15] Even when the other conditions for a just revolution
seem to be present, unless the revolutionary party has limited its violent
techniques it is acting inherently immorally, as well as weakening the chance
that the humane goals of the revolution will be realized. The very act of
reasoning about just revolutions implies the acceptance of violence as a
necessary tool, but it does not mean that violence is blessed or romanticized.

What exists in most of the world outside of the Atlantic Community,
the Soviet Union, and Japan are conditions of human indignity and degradation
beyond our comfortable imaginations. The conditions are intolerable, or soon
will be with increasing population. The political structures by and large are
not responsive to the social pressures. There will be revolutions. One of
the prerequisites in many countries for any progress toward justice is a re-
arrangement of the political structures in favor of the dispossessed. The
U. S. has a chance to move away from its blind opposition to revolutions and
from military support for reactionary regimes. The country will need guidance

as to which revolutionary movements to support. Part of the resources brought
to bear in the discussion of which revolutions to support will be reflection
from our traditions of social ethics.

Decisions about revolutions cannot, of course, be made only by
philosophers. The historical contingencies will be more important than
analysis and moral philosophy. The decision will be made under pressure and
in the light of the best judgments about the situation. Often the judgments
in Washington, D. C. will be made on the basis of misinformation (witness the
decision to intervene in the Dominican Republic). The task of one interested
in American morality is to criticize present U. S. militarism toward revolutionary movements, to expose the current romantic nonsense about revolution,
and to establish guidelines for American thought about revolutions.

X. THE THEOLOGY OF LIBERATION

In Latin America a group of theologians is working on conjoining in a new way the essence of their faith with the politics they believe to be necessary for the salvation of the poor in their countries. The group is in part dependent on the work of Ernst Bloch, Jürgen Moltmann, and Wolfhart Pannenberg in Europe. In particular they lean upon these Europeans for insight into the political consequences of hope, utopianism, and for connections between Marxism and Christianity. However, the fact that they are doing indigenous theology for Latin America gives their work its own distinctive traits. Catalino G. Arevalo of Manila has noted some similar trends in Asian theology, but again the Asian situation distinguishes its theology from that of Latin America. There also are parallels in black theologies of liberation in the United States. The Catholic heritage of Latin America, though, in this the only continent of the unindustrialized world which is overwhelmingly Christian, makes it quite different from black theologies in the United States.

This group which we can refer to as the theologians of liberation is a definite minority in a continent where the church is still largely associated with the status quo. They have not yet achieved the prominence in their society of either the social gospel movement or Christian realism in the periods of their dominance in the United States. In some ways, though the theologians are very concerned to speak to the poor and to the powerful, they are as of yet speaking largely to leftist Christians.

The group includes diverse figures. It seems to include on the moderate side Dom Helder Camaro, the Archbishop of Recife, well known in the United States for several books in English. Rubem Alvez, a Protestant professor at Sao Paulo, is also known in the United States from his teaching

at Union Theological Seminary and particularly for the influence of his A

Theology of Human Hope. Less well known in the United States is the work of

Gustavo Gutierrez, professor at the Catholic University of Peru, whose A

Theology of Liberation[1] has recently been translated. His influence is prob-

ably the most important in Latin America of any in the group. The work of

Juan Luis Segundo, of Uruguay, is very important and the translation and pub-

lication[2] of his works recently means that he will become well known in the

United States. Hugo Assmann, a Brazilian, may be the most politically radi-

cal of the group under consideration. The papers from the Medellin Conference

of 1968 are also representative of the fruits of many like-minded churchmen

who have been pushing their churches, Protestant and Catholic, to take his-

torical life seriously.

Theology for Gutierrez is critical reflection on the practice of

Christians. Theology as an act of reflecting consequently contributes to the

changing of the world. The task of theology is no longer to be primarily a

contribution to spiritual wisdom growing out of meditation or to rational

knowledge discovered through the synthesis of faith and philosophy. Practice

in Gutierrez's English edition is rendered as praxis to emphasize the Marxist

connotations of active world-transforming involvement. Theology is about the

transforming of both philosophy and the world.

In the Latin American context of massive deprivation theology reflects

upon Christian involvement in the effort to change the structures. It is

reflection upon the liberation-development controversy in Latin America.

Gutierrez's theology comes down wholeheartedly on the liberation side of the

debate. Development is associated with capitalist, evolutionary schemes of

adjustment within the system of dependency which characterizes Latin America.

Liberation denotes to Gutierrez the break with the system of domination by
the industrial world. It implies socialist revolutionary change as opposed
to the developmental ideology. Though Gutierrez does not explicitly bother
to isolate and discuss the Alliance for Progress, it is clear that his thought
is directed against both the implication of North American domination through
alliance of the southern countries and the implication of the preference for
progress through evolution rather than break through revolution.

Gutierrez, whom Arevalo has referred to as the "father of the leftist
Christians," shares features of the social theologies of both the social
gospel movement and the Christian realists. His thought is characterized by
the sense of social solidarity and hope or optimism of the social gospel.
However, his social model approximates closer to that of the conflict model
of the Christian realists than it does to the consensus-evolution model of
the social gospel. As in Karl Marx, revolution is the key to change. His
optimism and his realism are held together by the belief that revolutionary
change is necessary and that it can produce a new society and a new humanity.
Whether revolution can bear the weight he puts upon it would demand more careful examination of particular revolutions than his work undertakes. It is
only fair to note that he is working as a theologian, however, and that he
cannot be expected to do the complete job of the social scientist. He does
indicate that, though faith suggests norms and ways of evaluating political
actions, political science and philosophy are needed. "To be really effective, these options ought to be based on rational analyses of reality."[4]
This suggestion would indicate that, although his volume does not itself provide the structure between faith and political action, he is not opposed to
that being done in terms of social ethics and political philosophy.

Theology of Response and Transformation

The task of the theology of liberation according to Gutierrez is to examine the theological motifs of the Christian faith in the light of this historical situation of exploitation and dependence. Consequently the gospel news of the Kingdom of God on the one hand and the suffering of the people on the other are the grounds of his reflection.

Various developments in theological thinking have contributed to the development of the theology of liberation. Gutierrez credits as important: (1) The rediscovery of charity as "the center of the Christian life," (2) the focus on the need for a spirituality of the laity which relates to their work in the world, (3) the increased interest in Christian anthropology, (4) the intensity of the study of the church as a theological source, (5) the dialogue with Marxism, and (6) the renewed importance of eschatology as it has led to a revival of "the central role of historical praxis."[5]

The theology is characteristically responsive, that is it is reflection upon the preaching and acting of the church. Theology follows action, but it shares in the transforming role as it interprets the ultimate meaning of the events. It studies the events and the faith for the end of clarifying the Christian's commitments and goals. Finally, for this theology the meaning is found only in the continuing historical action.[6] At this point Gutierrez shares and quotes Schillebeeckx's conclusion: "The hermeneutics of the Kingdom of God consists especially in making the world a better place. Only in this way will I be able to discover what the Kingdom of God means."[7] The theology is reflection, but by the quality of its critical analysis it attempts to become part of the transformation of the world.

Development and Liberation

While admitting that poor peoples have had their hopes grouped around the concept development, Gutierrez is disappointed in the connotations of the term. Admittedly it has many meanings ranging from sheer economic growth to humanistic meanings. However, the programs of the developmentalists have in his judgment raised greater hopes than fulfillment. They have presupposed the continuing domination of Latin America by Europe and the United States. <u>Developmentalism</u> has for the theologians of liberation become synonymous with half-hearted reform measures, social evolution, and capitalism. Development has been seen as implying the success of the developed countries and the primitiveness of the undeveloped countries. Latin Americans are not at all sure that they wish to imitate the exploitive patterns of North America. Perhaps the central fiction of the developmentalist ideology was that societies developed independently of their international relations. The liberationist theologians now see that their underdevelopment is a prerequisite of the developed industrial countries. Perhaps the greatest conceptual shift from development to liberation thinking rests on this concept. The world is interrelated and the raw material-producing countries' poverty is directly related to the industrialized countries' wealth. So now the liberation theologians argue not that "The poor will always be with you," but that the poor are getting poorer because the rich are getting richer.

Gutierrez uses the term <u>liberation</u> to refer to three processes which he believes characterize history. <u>Liberation</u> refers to the conflict between oppressed peoples and their masters and summarizes the aspirations of the poor. It also means the process by which humanity fulfills its creative role and assumes "responsibility for [its] own destiny."[9] Finally, <u>liberation</u> is the victory over sin. Sin being understood as the lack of fraternity, justice, freedom, and equality because of the break between God and humanity

and among people. Gutierrez's intention is to present these three meanings

of <u>liberation</u> as "three levels of meaning of a single, complex process."[10]

Latin American Reality

The chapter on "The Process of Liberation in Latin America"[11] is sur-

prisingly short. It points again to the fact that despite Gutierrez's

attempt to become historical his writing remains a far distance from economics

and politics. It is in this chapter that one would expect to find either data

on exploitation or references to experiences of anguish and detailed analyses

of hopeful movements. The critique of developmentalism deepens the earlier

critique of the same subject. The theory of development is accused of having

ignored political factors or of seeming to ignore them in the interest of the

wealthy nations. The relationship of dependence in which the wealth of the

center depends upon the poverty of the periphery is asserted. The theoreti-

cal understanding of this relationship of dependence is regarded as unfinished

and more work on the problem is requested.

The revolutionary process which Gutierrez has in mind is one which

will "embrace the whole continent." The path of this revolutionary process

is not clear and the author admits it to be a "complex and changing situa-

tion." The urgency of the situation demands steps toward liberation but

Guiterrez's work reveals few steps in detail other than the process of Paulo

Freire's "pedagogy of the oppressed." The process of conscientization seems

to be his final word for the task of liberation at the present time. It is

the task of bringing to the people a new consciousness of their exploited

situation and a determination to do something about it. For Marx, the parallel

movement would be teaching or actions which increased class consciousness and

resulted in class solidarity. Perhaps in this enthusiasm for "conscientization"

we see the present agenda of the theologians of the left and also the purpose
of this book. It itself is a contribution to awaken Christians to their
obligation to commitment and action on behalf of the oppressed. Certainly in
its English translation, it is a call to increase the acuteness of the consciousness of North American Christians of the cost of their wealth to Latin
Americans. The conclusion the North American reader would draw from the
chapter on liberation in Latin America would be, mistakenly, that the process
is not far advanced.

The wrestling with the church is more thorough than the casual com-
ments about the revolutionary movements. This emphasis for a theologian is
appropriate from a certain perspective. If every institution must be internally subverted and reordered before anything resembling liberation can take
place, then the theologian needs to focus on the church. Gutierrez, however,
focuses on the church because this is where the faith is incarnated. Social
theologies which neglect the social institution which gave them birth are
doomed to exist in a rarefied intellectual world. Theology is the ideology
for the party called the church. He very carefully details the progress of
the Roman Catholic Church as it moves away from its previous positions. He,
of course, is not optimistic about his church adopting wholeheartedly the
theology of liberation, but he can detail a lot of movement toward historical
responsibility. He pleads with his church to throw off its colonial mentality
and to articulate an indigenous theology which will relate to a continent in
revolution. He asks for the church to throw its prestige and power behind
the movements for social transformation of Latin America. He knows that the
church which he is asking to become revolutionary is in fact part of the establishment. He sees in the church, however, "a growing radicalization" and
that positions which the church takes are more realistic and less ambiguous
than they were previously.[12]

Richard J. Neuhaus has raised the question of Christians acting as chaplains to various sides of the social struggle. He obviously deplored Roman Catholic prelates or Protestant preachers blessing United States armies in Vietnam. He suggests that Gutierrez, who is a chaplain to the National Union of Catholic University Students, has fallen into the trap of too uncritically blessing one side of the struggle. Neuhaus suggests the church is the place where real differences can be celebrated. Gutierrez asks the church to make a partisan commitment. Neuhaus concludes his critique by writing: "One's impression is that Gutierrez's vision is not that of the Church renewed but simply that of the Church switching sides."[13] Neuhaus has a point, but in the case of Gutierrez he may have pushed it too hard. Gutierrez does not bless any particular party in the book; his thought ranges all over Latin America. Obviously his thought is leftist in inclination and Marxist-Christian in social analysis. He pushes the church toward revolutionary involvement and away from colonial relationships. He pushes for indigenous social ownership of industry, rather than foreign capitalist control, but such broad stands seem to be quite different in the Latin American context from narrow partisan churchmanship. Regarding this question, his very vagueness about the revolutionary movements which earlier was seen as a defect of the book saves him from Neuhaus' criticism. His attitude toward a capitalist wanting to stay in communion in the church he would like to see evolve would certainly be no more radical than Jesus' supposed attitude toward Zealots or tax collectors joining his band of disciples. The capitalist past would be understood, as I assume the Zealots past or tax collecting background was compassionately regarded, as something that was past. As far as that issue is concerned one would be startled indeed to learn that advocates of the American war in Vietnam continued as enthusiastic supporters of The Reverend Neuhaus' ministry

in Brooklyn. Christian politics divides no less clearly than Christian
theology divides.

The Kingdom of God and Politics

Gutierrez suggests that the theology which focused on correct belief
emphasized the virtue of faith. The liberal, anthropological theology emphasized love and degenerated in Geuerbach and the death of God theologies. He
sees the current emphasis being placed upon hope. In all responsible Christian
theologies hope, faith and love are all present, but the emphasis can vary and
exhibit important consequences. In German philosophy he sees the movement
from faith in Hegel's thought to love in Feuerbach's and on to hope in Marx's
thought. The suggested movement is, of course, over simple, but it indicates
a movement that the theology of liberation joins. In Latin America, the
objective, empirical signs of social improvement through evolution, elections,
industrialization, or revolution are not overwhelming. Despair in the face of
tyranny and poverty is always an option. Part of freedom is to refuse to
despair and instead to hope. The gospel informs Christians of a gift of a new
reality, the Kingdom of God. This gift means to the theologians of liberation
that injustice will be overcome in history. The poor are blessed because their
poverty will be overcome and in their suffering and the overcoming of that
suffering rests the meaning of this history.

Latin America has been caught in the past; its hope rests in turning
to the future. However, Gutierrez and his allies emphasize, more than do
their European counterparts in the theologians of hope, that this vision of
the future must help transform the present. It is clear in Gutierrez's
thought that this influence that the future has upon the present is a human
work. Humanity trusting in promises of a better future is able to remake
the present into a more human condition.

"The Kingdom of God is a gift."[14] This gift is received in history; it has begun, but it is not complete. The meaning of the Kingdom is not clear in Gutierrez, but one must concede that it was not clear in The New Testament either. It is for Gutierrez a present reality which implies the need for the church as the nurturer and proclaimer of the Kingdom to be about the elimination of poverty and injustice. It is also for him the fulfillment of human development. Therefore, it is not to be confused with any stage of human development. He warns against confusing the Kingdom with revolution[15] or even with a just society.[16] Apparently the realization of the Kingdom is beyond the revolution in a just society where all are existing in a state which "opens up the promise and hope of complete communion of all men with God." The Kingdom is the merging of eternity and politics.[17] The lack of development of the concept of the Kingdom is perhaps due to his emphasis upon utopia.

Utopia is a positive term for Gutierrez. He claims a continuity with Thomas More's Utopia. He, however, moves beyond More's use of utopia to criticize society. He regards utopian thinking as projections of imaginative possibilities. He writes of utopia as both denunciation and annunciation. It is this projective feature of utopian thought that has earned it the criticism of realists who have regarded vision as often dangerous in a violent history. The subversive feature of the present is clearer than the constructive features of utopian thinking. In both Plato's Republic and More's Utopia the contemporary order was criticized, but there is very scant evidence that either regarded their dreams as models for political action. Gutierrez's work seems to give his blessing to utopian thought in general. At one level this cannot be criticized; the need for imagination in a technological rational systems-oriented world is clear. On the other hand, utopian thinking may be dangerous as well as creative. Perhaps if his emphasis upon praxis is given weight then it is not the impossible "no where" of the _Utopia_ that

is required, but strategies for achieving aspects of our hopes that are needed.

Gutierrez distinguishes between utopia and ideology; we also need to distin-

guish between utopia and relevant plans.

The reservations about Gutierrez's discussion of eschatology and poli-

tics do not invalidate his primary thesis. A preference for an emphasis upon

the Kingdom of God and a de-emphasis upon utopia only reinforces his argument.

He is never profounder than when he asserts:

> Faith and political action will not enter into a
> correct and fruitful relationship except through an
> effort to create a new type of person in a different
> society . . .[18]

Utopian thinking in its critical function is in some situations a useful tool,

but it is not the primary key to a better future. Christian thinking can use

or not use the tools of utopian thinking, just as it can use or refuse to use

the equipment of violent revolutionary theory. The vision of the Kingdom of

God is the indispensable symbol in Christian political thought.

The realism discussed in previous chapters is weak here at this point

where the theology of liberation is strong. Realism did not emphasize suffi-

ciently the possibilities of a new humanity in a new society and those possi-

bilities are essential to keep Christian political thinking from becoming

reactionary and defensive.

Freedom

Alves' _A Theology of Human Hope_ develops the discussion of freedom

more thoroughly than Gutierrez's work. In fact each chapter title of Alves'

work contains the term freedom. His first contribution to the discussion of

freedom is to root it solidly in the world proletariat's word of negation to

their rulers. Human freedom starts in this capacity to begin to live freely by the denial of the oppressor's will.[19] He moves beyond the system of existentialism because he believes it basically is conceived only with subjective freedom or an escape from the world.[20] Barth's theology is bypassed because temporality seems to Alves to have been annulled by the resurrection. History in Barth is settled and consequently in Alves' perspective neither free nor interesting.[21] Moltmann too, in Alves' judgment, sees the future as already finished.[22] The theology of liberation insists that the present is not finished but that it is a horizon which is filled out of the labors resulting from faithfulness to promises in a suffering present.

The language of humanistic Marxism, disguised in Alves under the rubric of humanist messianism, nearly achieves a satisfactory understanding and practice of freedom. However, it falls short, Alves argues, as it only roots its hopes in what is calculable. This hardly seems to be an adequate critique of Marxism, in that it has many other problems, and also because Karl Marx's own hopes often bypassed any scientific calculation of which he was capable. It is simply not true that only messianic humanism, Alves' form of theology, can provide confidence in the future beyond the empirical data or scientific theory available. However, such an argument is an internal matter for Alves to worry about in his attempts to distinguish his theology from Marxist sociology.[23]

Both Marxism and the theology of liberation perceive history as the arena of human freedom. The dynamics of that history are understood differently as their own histories are different. Alves summarizes the movement of liberation as threefold. By his statement he makes it clear that for him freedom comes through revolution. First, the old oppresses the new force which denies its hegemony. Second, the new life uses power against the oppressor (in Marx's terms the negation of the negation or revolution).

Third, the new expresses itself in creativity and experimentation.[24] Freedom

is the capacity to, in the present, fulfill one's capacity to be human by

acting to create a new future. This is possible in many ways, but in Latin

America the primary motif will be through pro-revolutionary actions. Freedom

is the act of defiance, the act of winning over oppression, and the act of

building new places for freedom. As with Gutierrez this unifies salvation or

liberation and political action.

In Latin America, one of the forces preventing liberation is the power

from North America expressed in all sorts of treaties, understandings,

cultural domination, and economic relationships. Alves turns to Reinhold

Niebuhr to explain in Augustinian terms how the powerful pridefully justify

their self-interested domination in moral rationalizations.[25] These rational-

izations backed by financial arrangements and military force press in upon

the weaker Latin Americans and prevent their movement toward freer community.

The powerful try to maintain their position; that implies status quo policies

or at least policies permitting only evolutionary changes. In Alves' thought,

the powerful and rich are unable to engage in thorough-going change because

their interest lies in making the future only an enlargement of the past.

National interest rather than justice is in turn perceived as what serves eco-

nomic, military, and prestige interests.[26] This policy is expressed in Latin

America as North American counterrevolutionary power.

The theologians of liberation are quite frank that the imperial rela-

tions in which their countries exist are a major part of their problem.

However, as a group they are strangely not vociferously anti-North American.

This may permit North American Christians to learn from their Southern broth-

ers so that the extent to which the United States is hindering the work of

health or salvation in Latin America may be seen. Such a perception, including the need for revolutionary change in Latin America, helps United States citizens see the horror of our counterrevolutionary policies.

Gutierrez concluded his impressive study of the theology of liberation by asserting that all of the theologies were not equivalent in value to real acts promoting liberation. Solidarity with the exploited is required of Christians. In Latin America, in Uruguay and Chile[27] in particular, that solidarity has been expressed in Marxist-Christian political alliances. The North American corporate response has been to try to subvert these movements for liberation. The developing of ways to control the multi-national corporate giants[28] and to prevent the anti-democratic practices of companies like International Telephone and Telegraph in Chile is part of the North American Christian's task as an act of solidarity with his brothers and sisters in the South.

XI. THE KINGDOM OF GOD AND COUNTERREVOLUTION

The argument of the book has suggested that, though the contemporary
church seems to be without a program and is suffering from directionless
drift, it has a mission. That task is the proclamation of the coming of God's
Kingdom and the engagement of its members in the work of that Kingdom. It has
by looking briefly at the ministry of Jesus, Gregory VII, Luther and John Knox
suggested that "The Kingdom is not only God acting; it is God acting in a
situation of conflict."[1] The church's capture by the middle class deflected
its energies from its world transforming role and led to the critique of its
foundations by Karl Marx. In the United States the Kingdom, though variously
interpreted, has been central to the evolution of Christian thought. It was
interpreted by Rauschenbusch in an American version as connected with democracy
and socialism. The realist critique of the social gospel movement shattered
the confidence in evolution producing the Kingdom and revealed the conflictual
character of human development. Though the Kingdom was a norm, its realization was understood symbolically as both the fulfillment and the end of human
history. The Latin American theologians have expressed their social theology
in hopeful terms reminiscent of the social gospel, but their model of social
development has been that of conflict and in particular of revolution. Revolution and hope are brought together in a fresh synthesis growing out of the
Latin American Christian-Marxist dialogue. The discussion of revolution has
concluded that, while the counterrevolutionary fanaticism of the United States
is inappropriate in the developing world, romanticism about revolution also
is misleading. This leads to the conclusion that part of the task of
Christians in the United States is to deflect the nation/state from its present

counterrevolutionary course. This argument will be made in terms drawn from political and social analysis before giving a closing word about the politics of the Kingdom of God.

The subtitle of Henry Kissinger's major work summarizes the drift of United States' foreign policy since World War II, "The Politics of Conservatism in a Revolutionary Age." The United States has been engaged in buttressing conservative regimes in every continent of the world. In part this was justified by the character of the militant tyranny of Stalinist society in the Soviet Union. To a degree, it was inevitable because the United States found itself entrenched around the world at the conclusion of World War II. Also, it was for economic reasons, because the industrial plant of the United States required raw materials from around the world. In addition, the capitalism of the United States involved the country in the economies of most of the peoples of the non-communist world. The counterrevolutionary fervor of the United States was rooted in its anti-communism. Several forces conspired to produce the violent forms of anti-communism which dominated American life. The myths of a revolutionary ideology of its own in democratic freedom and equality were threatened by the communist myths. The revived capitalism of post-World War II America necessarily feared the economic theory and practice of the state capitalism of the Soviet Union and its empire which masqueraded under the name of communism. The revolution in China broke American understandings of its own special role in China. The religious sensitivity of the American population was threatened by the religious atheism of Marxism. Refugee populations from Europe and Cuba fed the fears of communism. The claim to leadership of the world revolutions by the tyranny of Stalinist Moscow was believed in the United States and this called forth the counterrevolutionary politics.

The theme of counterrevolution is present in all the post-World War II presidents and secretaries of state. It is present in differing degrees, of course, and it does not reach the extremes in those sophisticated leaders that it did in Christian anti-communist movements, the McCarthy extremists, the John Birch Society, etc. From Acheson through Kissinger the assumption that America must be a power in the world to protect its interests, prestige, and allies is found. Those interests include economic interests dependent upon the status quo and an ideology couched in anti-communist terminology. Acheson muted his ideology or hid it under pragmatic choices, but even his speech at Amherst revealed a commitment to anti-communism under the guise of defending freedom. John Foster Dulles was more explicit about developing an ideology of freedom to counter the ideology of communism. His rhetoric fed the fires of anti-communism; however, in practice he was more cautious than either the preceding or following democratic administrations in risking war with communist forces. He talked tough but used his big stick quite sparingly. The Kennedy presidency was characterized by bold rhetoric in Berlin and Washington and in counterrevolutionary gestures in the Alliance for Progress. Its performance at the Bay of Pigs, Laos, and Vietnam was less bold, but in the Cuban missile crisis it seemed to return to Dulles' brinksmanship. Johnson led the country in supporting the successor to Trujillo in the Dominican Republic against the liberals and into the quagmire of Vietnam for which all the administrations since World War II had prepared the path. Nixon's rhetoric and action in Southeast Asia revealed his commitment to the ideology of anti-communism even as changing world realities were expressed in his bold attempts to formalize a growing detente.

Throughout the period, collaboration with the governments of South Africa, Greece, Portugal, Spain, Pakistan, Iran, military aid to most anti-communist nations, subversion in many areas of the world, the rhetoric of American politics, and economic practice were all built into this overall posture of counterrevolution. The nation trying to protect its own revolutionary goal of liberty and claiming a belief in equality found itself allied with racism in South Africa, fascism in Spain and Portugal, with medieval feudal arrangements in Latin America, and French imperialism in Southeast Asia.

Constitutional government in its mass form is a relatively recent arrival in human history. It is hidden in the struggles of the seventeenth and eighteenth centuries of European peoples and in its American expression. In many ways it is the adjustment of classical conservative forms of government to liberal movements and philosophies. In the twentieth century it is threatened most by fascism and communism. Tribalism, feudalism, and various other systems impede attempts to transplant it elsewhere. It probably is most appropriate or at least best maintained in societies influenced by the traditions out of which it grew. One significant question is, can it survive its struggle with fascism and communism? Obviously it can survive the conflict with communism only through accommodation and detente. Then the question is reshaped to question whether it can survive the policies necessary to urge communist countries to detente. How many alliances with tyranny can be endured and supported without constitutional government in the United States cracking beyond all recognition?

The struggle with fascism in Europe and its Japanese form in Asia left the United States in its hegemonic role. The struggle with communism combined with economic motivations has kept the United States in this role up to the present. The United States has insisted upon and received extraterritorial privileges in the form of military bases around the world in a

form and to an extent never before matched in the history of the world.
This occupation of much of the world coupled with the drive of United States
industrialism has been producing changes around the world. In fact, it has
unleashed forces comparable in their fury in remaking traditional society to
the counter thrusts of Marxist revolutionaries. This capitalist-military
thrust has been reinforced by the ideology of American minds into a movement
that has been called a revolution without either Marx or Jesus. The costs
of the strain of this movement on the United States has been documented by
Seymour Melman.[3] The willingness of the United States to shoulder immense
defense budgets for its anti-communist ideology has permitted the development
of more solid economies in Japan and Europe. So that at the present time the
economic future of the United States, though not desperate, is shaky and the
question of successful reconversion to peace-time economy very difficult.

The problem of the counterrevolutionary stance of the United States
involves every aspect of American life. The problem is at its heart an issue
of spirit. It is a question of the spirit of the American people as expressed
in foreign policy. The major driving force behind the American counterrevolutionary force is the ideology of anti-communism. Anti-communism is a
pseudo-theological or ideological problem playing on the deepest fears,
insecurities and hopes of the American people. It is, moreover, an issue
with which the churches and the schools could deal effectively if they understood and were willing to risk some security.

The major lesson of the Vietnam war ought to be that a policy of
counterrevolution is a disaster. Robert L. Heilbroner, an economist with
Asian wartime experience, has argued that the primary purpose of the United
States in Vietnam was to demonstrate that wars of national liberation would
be defeated. It was necessary to prove that the road of revolution was a

"disaster for the revolutionaries."[4] Perhaps just the opposite has been proven as the United States threw away its moral prestige and polluted its reservoir of world good will in its futile Asian war.

The leadership of the churches learned through the Vietnam war that more than a particular policy was bankrupt. The assumptions underlying the whole foreign policy stance have been seen as mistaken. The hint that counter-revolutionary policies in a changing world finally are in error is contained in a National Council of Churches statement on the Vietnam war.

> A national repentance is required. This means reexamin-
> ing and changing basic ideas, positions and policies about
> this war beginning in the minds of church members. This
> urgently means a new seriousness about negotiation. It means
> repenting of some habitual assumptions: that American power
> must be used for ideological purposes, that America alone
> must "keep the peace," that military power is the chief means
> of keeping the peace, that peace is best served by backing
> the status quo.[5]

The French, Russian and Chinese revolutions all displaced the system of international relations and called forth reactions from status quo powers. Major actors in the international system cannot go through massive-violent disruption without producing counteraction from the other actors in the sys-tem. The French revolution was both betrayed from within France and defeated by the status quo powers which symbolized that victory at the Congress of Vienna. The Russian revolution has been betrayed from within and turned into something far different from the revolutionaries' goals, but the inter-national system has adjusted to live with this new status quo power. The Chinese revolution has demonstrated little ability to export its Chinese-Marxist ideology and the system seems able to adjust to its presence. There will continue to be numerous national revolutions throughout the world and many of these will be new mixtures of Marxism and nationalism. They need not affect the international system in a major way unless the status quo powers intervene and make them issues for the whole system.

Russian or Chinese involvement in revolutions in Latin America or American involvement in revolutions in Southern Africa could, however, again disrupt the evolution of the international system toward detente. The detente if achieved among Europe, China, the U.S.S.R., Japan, and the U. S. can be a relatively secure detente because of the presence of nuclear weapons. The future holds the promise of an increasingly secure detente reinforced by the threat of nuclear terror coupled with revolutions which can either be kept localized or expanded to threaten this emerging agreement. The above recognition of the stability introduced by nuclear terror is not to suggest acquiescence in nuclear stalemate, but just to recognize that in present history nuclear weapons play an ambiguous role of promising both security and the end of all security.

The emerging picture of security among the super powers and convulsion in the developing world requires, however, that the super powers exercise restraint. The restraint will have to be mutual. In the world of international politics there is little to guarantee that mutuality, but there are deep signs of both the Soviet Union and China becoming status quo powers. The evolution of the United States to a position joining the other powers depends on its surrendering its tendency to react in counterrevolutionary ways.

The major thrust of U. S. counterrevolutionary power was, of course, in Indochina where in the name of anti-communism and the defeat of a war of national liberation the United States engaged itself from the 1950 support of the French forces to evacuation in 1975.

The second major arena has been in Latin America where the United States has intervened consistently against revolutionary movements.

Especially noteworthy are the C.I.A. subversion and overthrow of the left-
wing regime of Arbenz in Guatamala under Allen Dulles in 1954, the Bay of
Pigs invasion of 1961 under Kennedy's leadership, the cooperation with the
forces that overthrew President Goulart of Brazil in 1964, the suppression
of the liberal forces in the Dominican revolution of 1965 under President
Johnson's administration, and the defeat of Allende in Chile by Kissinger.
In all cases fear of communism combined with U. S. business interests to
favor the less revolutionary party. In addition to many more specific actions
of direct intervention, two major programs reinforced the conservative policy
of the United States.

The Alliance for Progress, conceived as an antidote to Cuban-sponsored
revolution in Latin America, was reformist oriented. It assumed that progress
in Latin America was to be made through social evolution along democratic and
capitalist lines. The program assumed a viability in democratic procedures
for changing the social system which had never been demonstrated. Democratic
procedures in the Western world had been won through revolution, but in Latin
America revolution was regarded as too dangerously Marxist and so it was
argued that through democratic procedures the oligarchies would surrender
their feudal privileges. The Kennedy rhetoric of peaceful change was followed
in the Johnson administration by the policies of Thomas Mann who gave up even
the pretense of favoring progressive development. Important capital funds
have been transferred to Latin America by various unilateral and multilateral
programs for funding economic development.[6] These funds, however, are subject
to all the entangling relationships involved in dealing with United States
financial interests. The funds transferred for development have not equaled
the funds taken out of these countries in profits, raw materials, and repay-
ment on loans. So in the Alliance there was a senior partner and a host of

smaller allies. Progress did not result, and the arrangement is seen more and more as a relationship which kept Latin America in a dependent relationship. The refusal of the Nixon administration to begin to reconceive this relationship was symbolized by John Irwin's negative reply to the developing nations' plea for a new status at the UNCTAD Conference in Santiago in 1971. The forces for change in Latin America no longer think in terms of an alliance with the U. S., but rather they conceive of the relationship as one of the exploited and the exploitor.

If the United States policy of peaceful alliance for social change is seen mostly as a rhetorical policy, its other policy is very real. Along with the articulation of a policy of peaceful change the Kennedy administration deepened U. S. involvement in counter-insurgency warfare. Military assistance since World War II has been given to eighty-five nations and in one year, 1967, the United States was involved in training soldiers from sixty different countries.[7] Most of the armies of Latin America received training in both regular warfare and counter-insurgency tactics. Advisors and equipment were dispatched to many countries which were experiencing internal difficulties with political insurgents. The sale and gift of military hardware by the United States to Latin America, the accompanying training, and the combat support of U. S. advisors has not forced the United States into anything threatening to become another Vietnam. However, the potential is always there. The Nixon doctrine was designed to prevent the United States from engaging its major forces except under specific conditions which are not likely to occur in Latin America. U. S. policy, however, continues to engage U. S. wealth and personnel against revolution in Latin America.

The 1972 presidential election revealed the dangers of supporting counterrevolutionary moves abroad. The same corporation which negotiated with

the Central Intelligence Agency for the suppression of an elected socialist
regime in Chile was exposed as involved in corrupting the Republican party
in the United States. The exposure of ITT's arrangements with the Republican
party forced the party first to give up its San Diego convention site to move
to Miami. Further exposure unveiled Justice Department irregularities in
dropping prosecution of ITT in antitrust suits in return for campaign contributions. Corporations which develop tactics for subverting governments
abroad in the name of securing their investments are not going to be engaged
in defending the public's interest in representative government at home. The
arbitrary power U. S. corporations develop in dealing with weak nation states
is expressed in internal U. S. politics by a capriciousness and disregard for
public virtue which undermines democratic government.

     The Nixon administration and its reelection committee used in the
domestic political situation tools and methods developed for fighting revolution abroad. The majority of those convicted in the Watergate scandal had
received their political training in the Central Intelligence Agency's anti-
Castro operations. There is a dividing line between covert operations conducted by the CIA for purposes abroad and domestic politics. However, the
"Dirty Tricks" operation of the Committee to Reelect the President broke down
that dividing wall. Fears by responsible people involved in resisting criticism of cold-war policy resulted in tactics designed for the cold war being
used to corrupt the national political scene. Senator McGovern's policies
concerning the war in Vietnam were seen to be so dangerous by those still
lingering in the mood of the anti-communist spirit that they betrayed the
American political process. Earlier revelations concerning the CIA in the
democratic administration of Johnson had proven that the CIA did in fact
intervene in supporting domestic groups even though forbidden to do so by law.

In case after case, from the Harrisburg trial of alleged conspirators to the Ellsburg trial, government complicity in illegal means of prosecution were proven.

The complicity of the United States in fixing elections and political processes abroad in support of its counterrevolutionary policies is generally known. The possibility that the alliances with dictators and the conduct of counterrevolutionary warfare by the United States may unleash forces which will end representative government in the United States must now be faced. The cost of the war in Vietnam will be borne for generations, and the fundamental disrespect for democratic procedures built into the CIA and FBI is a very dangerous force. William Appleman Williams put the issue directly in 1962, that unless the United States gave up its economic expansion accompanied by counterrevolutionary policies it would lose democracy.[8] He was hoping that the New Frontier policies would signal the changes he thought necessary. Ten years later we saw as gross an assault upon the electoral process by an administration as we have ever witnessed. The attack was carried out because of fears regarding foreign policy directions and the fears of the American business community which paid for the reelection campaign of the President. It is unclear whether or not some form of elected representative government could sustain itself in this country while continuing to oppose revolution around the world. It seems unlikely, but history reveals many ironical configurations. Regardless of the outcome domestically of the present stance toward radical social change it is a morally bankrupt policy. Change cannot come in many countries without revolution and the present situation is so degrading to human life that revolution is demanded. When people rise up to throw off unjust oligarchs, even if they do it in the name of Marx as well as Jesus, we have no responsibility nor right to protect the oligarchs.

Conclusion

The hope for the Kingdom of God is heard differently in various situations. If a culture is optimistically thinking it will realize utopia through
social engineering, it stands as a warning that the future is more complex
than human design. It stands as a warning against human prideful assertiveness. If a culture is despairing before intersecting crises, it promises a
more hopeful fulfillment than the pessimism of humanity. In our situation
the Kingdom is a symbol that the United States will not determine the future
of the world and that eventually the exploited peoples of the world will come
into their own destiny. The promise of the Kingdom, then, is one of judgment
on the proud and a sign of hope to the poor. The hope contained in it for
the powerful is largely that on the other side of repentance there is a task
of responsible building and planning which too is part of the Kingdom.

The response to the Kingdom is not primarily one of conceptualizing.
Matthew had it right when he wrote: "I tell you this: anything you did not
for one of these, however humble, you did not do for me."[9] Response is
judged by action, concrete actions of feeding, visiting, clothing, and caring.
Moltmann senses this imperative to active engagement as he concludes his work
on revolution: "We are construction workers and not only interpreters of the
future whose power in hope as well as in fulfillment is God. This means that
Christian hope is a creative and militant hope in history."[10]

Christian politics of the Kingdom have consequences in all the arenas
in which Christians find themselves. This study has focused on only one of
the struggles. The poor nations are trying to throw off the shackles of
oligarchies, corrupt officials, and foreign domination. Revolutions are brew-
ing and the danger exists that the United States will support the counterrevolutionary side in many of the struggles. If the theologians of liberation

are correct, as surely they are, justice demands revolution in many places. American support of pro-oligarchic counterrevolutionary policies in Latin America and pro-racist policies in Southern Africa is certainly foolish striving against the Kingdom of God. Those abroad and those in the United States who work to end the American fascination with conservative politics in a revolutionary age certainly are contributing to the building of the Kingdom of God. The revolutionaries abroad and their supporters in the United States can best serve the cause of their citizenship in the Kingdom by hopeful realistic action. The theologians of hope and liberation at their most political level have no quarrel with the Christian realists at their most hopeful point.

CHAPTER NOTES

CHAPTER II. THE KINGDOM OF GOD AS A POLITICAL MODEL OF HOPE

[1]Thomas S. Kuhn, The Structure of Scientific Revolutions (Chicago: University of Chicago Press, 1962).

[2]Jürgen Moltmann, Religion, Revolution and the Future (New York: Charles Scribner's Sons, 1969).

[3]Rubem Alves, A Theology of Human Hope (Washington: Corpus Books, 1969).

[4]Harvey Cox, The Feast of Fools (Cambridge: Harvard University Press, 1969).

[5]Michael Novak, A Theology for Radical Politics (New York: Herder and Herder, 1969).

[6]James Cone, Black Theology and Black Power (New York: Seabury Press, 1969).

[7]James Cone, A Black Theology of Liberation (Philadelphia: J. B. Lippincott Company, 1970).

[8]Michael Walzer, The Revolution of the Saints (New York: Atheneum, 1969).

[9]Wolfhart Pannenberg, Theology and the Kingdom of God (Philadelphia: The Westminster Press, 1969), p. 76.

[10]H. Richard Niebuhr, The Kingdom of God in America (New York: Harper & Brothers, 1937).

CHAPTER III. CHRISTIAN FAITH AND REVOLUTION

[1]Moltmann, Religion, Revolution and the Future, p. 136.

[2]Ibid., p. 137.

[3]S. G. F. Brandon, Jesus and the Zealots (New York: Charles Scribner's Sons, 1967), p. 1.

[4]Oscar Cullmann, Jesus and the Revolutionaries (New York: Harper and Row, Publishers, 1970).

[5]The entire discussion of the Gregorian revolution is totally dependent upon the late Eugen Rosenstock-Huessy, _Out of Revolution_ (New York: William Morrow and Company, 1938).

[6]_Ibid._, p. 518.

[7]_Ibid._, p. 521.

[8]_Ibid._

[9]_Ibid._, p. 523.

[10]_Ibid._, p. 528.

[11]_Ibid._, p. 537.

[12]_Ibid._, pp. 538-539.

[13]In Martin Luther, _Three Treatises_ (Philadelphia: Muhlenberg Press, 1960), pp. 3-111, underlining mine.

[14]E.g., Ernst Troeltsch, _The Social Teaching of The Christian Churches_, II (New York: Harper Torchbooks, 1931), or Paul Althaus, _The Ethics of Martin Luther_ (Philadelphia: Fortress Press, 1972), or A. G. Dickens, _Reformation and Society in Sixteenth Century Europe_ (London: Harcourt, Brace and World, Inc., 1966).

[15]John Dillenberger, _Martin Luther: Selections from His Writings_ (New York: Doubleday and Company, Inc., 1961), p. 365.

[16]Walzer, _The Revolution of the Saints_, p. 10. The discussion depends directly upon Walzer's study.

[17]_Ibid._, p. 109.

[18]_Ibid._, pp. 317-318.

[19]_Ibid._, p. 320.

[20]For the above discussion, in theme and detail, the author is in debt to Eugen Rosenstock-Huessy and Michael Walzer in the works cited.

[21]Rosemary Ruether, _The Radical Kingdom_ (New York: Harper & Row Publishers, 1970), pp. 16-17.

CHAPTER IV.   THE REVOLUTIONARY ANTI-KINGDOM OF KARL MARX

[1]Robert C. Tucker, _The Marxian Revolutionary Idea_ (New York: W. W. Norton & Co., 1969), p. 225.

[2]Karl Marx, "From Letter to Ferdinand Nieuwenhuis" (February 22, 1881) in Saul K. Padover, ed., On Revolution, The Karl Marx Library, I (New York: McGraw-Hill Book Company, 1971), p. 67.

[3]Alasdair C. Macintyre, Marxism: An Interpretation (London: SCM Press, Ltd., 1953).

[4]Karl Barth, "An Introductory Essay" in Ludwig Feuerbach, The Essence of Christianity (New York: Harper Torchbook, 1957), p. xxviii.

[5]Ibid., p. 73.

[6]Ibid., p. 195.

[7]Quoted by R. N. Carew Hunt, Marxism Past and Present (London: Geoffrey Bles, 1954), p. 28.

[8]Ibid., p. 32.

[9]Karl Marx, "Theses on Feuerback," A Handbook of Marxism (London: Victor Gollaney Ltd., 1937).

[10]The discussion of Marx's concept of alienation is dependent on John Plamenatz, Man and Society, II (London: Longmans, Green and Co., Ltd., 1963), and upon his lectures, Michelmas Term, 1965, Oxford University.

[11]Marx, "Early Philosophical Manuscripts," extract in T. B. Bottomore and Maximilien Rubel, Karl Marx Selected Writings in Sociology and Social Philosophy (Harmondsworth, Middlesex: Penguin Books, Ltd., 1963), p. 178.

[12]"We have, however, derived the concept of alienated labour (alienated life) from political economy, from an analysis of the movement of private property. But the analysis of this concept shows that although private property appears to be the basis and cause of alienated labour, it is rather a consequence of the latter, just as the gods are fundamentally not the cause but the product of confusions of human reason." Ibid., pp. 176-177.

[13]Ibid., p. 42.

[14]Reinhold Niebuhr, ed., Marx and Engels on Religion (New York: Schocken Books, 1964), pp. 41, 42.

[15]For example, Jean-Yves Calvez, La Pensée de Karl Marx (Paris: Editions Du Sevil, 1956), pp. 21-22.

[16]Marx, "On the Jewish Question," Selected Essays (London: Leonard Parsons, 1926), p. 97.

[17]Niebuhr, ed., Marx and Engels on Religion, p. 57.

[18]Ibid., pp. x, xi.

[19]Ibid., p. 67.

[20]Marx, Capital, I (London: J. M. Dent & Sons, Ltd., 1957), p. 269.

[21]Ibid., p. 259.

[22]Ibid., p. 283.

[23]Ibid.

[24]Ibid., II, p. 72.

[25]Eugene Kamenka, The Ethical Foundations of Marxism (London: Routledge and Kegan Paul, 1962), p. 29.

[26]"The revelation that Marx now (1844) experienced consisted in the discovery that the hidden meaning of Hegelianism lay in the realm of economics; Hegelianism was an economic theory in disguise." Louis J. Halle, "Marx's Religious Drama," Encounter (October, 1965), p. 34.

[27]Quoted by Kamenka, Ethical Foundations, p. 145.

[28]Frederich Engels, "Herr Eagen Duhrings Revolution in Science," E. Burns, ed., A Handbook of Marxism (London: Victor Gallancy, Ltd., 1937), p. 248.

[29]Kamenka, Ethical Foundations, p. 106.

[30]Quoted by H. B. Acton, The Illusion of the Epoch (London: Cohen and West, Ltd., 1955), p. 215.

[31]Marx, "On the Jewish Question," Leonard Parsons, ed., Selected Essays - Karl Marx (London: Leonard Parsons, 1926), p. 84.

[32]Bottomore and Rubel, eds., Selected Writings, p. 207.

[33]Ibid., p. 188.

[34]Robert C. Tucker, Philosophy and Myth in Karl Marx (Cambridge: University Press, 1961), p. 242.

[35]David McLellan, Marx's Grundrisse (London: The Macmillan Press, Ltd., 1971).

[36]Lewis S. Feuer, ed., Marx and Engels (Garden City: Anchor Books, 1959), p. 27.

[37]Ibid., p. 29.

[38]Ibid., p. 41.

[39]Ibid., p. 29.

[40]Reinhold Niebuhr, "Marx and Engels on Religion" in Ronald H. Stone, ed., _Faith and Politics_ (New York: George Braziller, 1968), pp. 33-46.

[41]Tucker, _The Marxian Revolutionary Idea_, p. 225.

[42]Frederick Engels, "Introduction" in Karl Marx, _The Civil War in France_ (New York: International Publishers, 1940), p. 22.

[43]_Ibid._, p. 7.

CHAPTER V. CHRISTIAN SOCIALISM AND THE KINGDOM OF GOD

[1]H. Richard Niebuhr, _The Kingdom of God in America_ (New York: Harper & Brothers Publishers, 1937).

[2]Quoted by C. Howard Hopkins, "An American Prophet," in Benjamin E. Mays, ed., _A Gospel for the Social Awakening, Selections from the Writings of Walter Rauschenbusch_ (New York: Association Press, 1950), p. 13.

[3]Walter Rauschenbusch, _Prayers of the Social Awakening_ (Boston: The Pilgrim Press, 1925), p. 18.

[4]_Ibid._, p. 139.

[5]Walter Rauschenbusch, _A Theology for the Social Gospel_ (New York: Abingdon Press, n.d.). Originally published by the Macmillan Company, 1917, p. 131.

[6]Walter Rauschenbusch, _The Righteousness of the Kingdom_ (Nashville: Abingdon Press, 1968), pp. 79-110.

[7]Rauschenbusch, _A Theology for the Social Gospel_, p. 146.

[8]_Ibid._, pp. 131-145.

[9]_Ibid._, p. 141.

[10]Max Stackhouse, "The Continuing Importance of Walter Rauschenbusch," in _The Righteousness of the Kingdom_, p. 35.

[11]_Ibid._, p. 34.

[12]Walter Rauschenbusch, _Christianity and the Social Crisis_ (Macmillan, Torchbook Edition, 1907; New York: Harper and Row Publishers, Inc., 1964), p. 371.

[13]Walter Rauschenbusch's praise for Henry George's land tax in _Christianizing the Social Order_ (New York: The Macmillan Company, 1912), p. 392, does not underlie the rest of his argument about the economic order. He never gave up on the land tax idea, but its role in his thought seems to have modified with events and with its decline in the popular mind. He stubbornly kept the idea as a source of reform and partially because he attributed his own social awakening in 1886 to "the agitation of Henry George."

[14]Stackhouse, "The Continuing Importance of Walter Rauschenbusch," p. 32.

[15]Rauschenbusch, _Christianity and the Social Crisis_, p. 369.

[16]_Ibid._, p. 408.

[17]_Ibid._, p. 412.

[18]_Ibid._, p. 414.

[19]See Robert D. Cross, "Introduction to the Torchbook Edition," _ibid_, pp. xvii-xix.

[20]_Ibid._, pp. 420-421.

CHAPTER VI.   THE DEVELOPMENT OF AMERICAN POLITICAL REALISM

[1]Raymond Aron, _Peace and War_ (New York: Doubleday and Company, 1966), p. 592.

[2]Hans J. Morgenthau, _Dilemmas of Politics_ (Chicago: University of Chicago Press, 1958), p. 51.   The discussion of the philosophy of Morgenthau is reprinted with changes from _Religion in Life_ (Autumn 1965), copyright © 1965 by Abingdon Press.

[3]Hans J. Morgenthau, _Politics Among Nations_ (New York: Alfred A. Knopf, 1958), p. 237.

[4]_Ibid._, p. 251.

[5]Morgenthau, _Dilemmas of Politics_, p. 374.

[6]Hans J. Morgenthau, "Reaction to the Van Doren Reaction," _New York Times Magazine_ (November 22, 1959), p. 17.

[7]Morgenthau, _Dilemmas of Politics_, p. 3.

[8]Morgenthau, _Politics Among Nations_, p. 259.

[9]Hans J. Morgenthau, _In Defense of the National Interest_ (New York: Alfred A. Knopf, 1951), p. 33.

[10]Hans J. Morgenthau, _Scientific Man vs. Power Politics_ (Chicago: University of Chicago Press, 1946), p. 181.

[11]_Ibid._, p. 186.

[12]Morgenthau, _Scientific Man_, p. 95.

[13]Hans J. Morgenthau, Lecture to International Fellows Program, Columbia University, February 23, 1962.

[14] Hans J. Morgenthau, "Love and Power," Commentary (March, 1962), pp. 247-251.

[15] Morgenthau, Scientific Man, p. 211.

[16] Hans J. Morgenthau, "Death in the Nuclear Age," Commentary (September, 1961), p. 234.

[17] Morgenthau, Scientific Man, p. 168.

[18] Ibid., p. 223.

[19] Hans J. Morgenthau, "Globalism, Johnson's Moral Crusade," The New Republic (June 3, 1965), p. 19.

[20] Reinhold Niebuhr, Hans J. Morgenthau and Richard Hudson, "The Ethics of War and Peace in the Nuclear Age," War/Peace (February, 1967), p. 3.

[21] Harry R. Davis and Robert C. Good, eds., Reinhold Niebuhr on Politics (New York: Charles Scribner's Sons, 1960), p. 333.

[22] This treatment is brief because I have compared the two thinkers elsewhere; Reinhold Niebuhr: Prophet to Politicians (Nashville: Abingdon Press, 1972), pp. 200-204.

[23] See Hans J. Morgenthau, Truth and Power: Essays of a Decade (London: Pall Mall Press, 1970), pp. 398-432; or Ronald H. Stone, Reinhold Niebuhr, pp. 191-195, 244.

[24] Hans J. Morgenthau, A New Foreign Policy for the United States (New York: Frederick A. Praeger, 1969).

[25] An example of this overly simple representation of Niebuhr's thought is Carl E. Braaten's unpublished paper, "Eschatological Ethics: Toward a Theory of Christian Ethics," given at the annual meeting of the American Society of Christian Ethics in Richmond (January, 1973).

[26] Reinhold Niebuhr, The Nature and Destiny of Man, II (New York: Charles Scribner's Sons, 1943), p. 308.

[27] Ibid., p. 286.

[28] Ibid., pp. 285-286.

[29] Ibid., p. 207.

[30] Ibid., p. 156.

CHAPTER VII. A PERSPECTIVE ON INTERNATIONAL POLITICS

[1] Kenneth N. Waltz, Man, the State and War (New York: Columbia University Press, 1965).

[2]In Horrace V. Harrison, ed., The Role of Theory in International Relations (Princeton: D. Van Nostrand Company, Inc., 1964), p. 98.

[3]Stanley H. Hoffmann, ed., Contemporary Theory in International Relations (Englewood Cliffs: Prentice-Hall, Inc., 1960), pp. 8-9.

[4]Kenneth W. Thompson, "Toward a Theory of International Politics," American Political Science Review (September, 1955), pp. 733-746.

[5]John Stoessinger, in a lecture to the International Fellows Program, Columbia University, May 1, 1964.

[6]Reinhold Niebuhr, Christian Realism and Political Problems (New York: Charles Scribner's Sons, 1953), pp. 15-31.

[7]Kenneth W. Thompson, Political Realism and the Crisis of World Politics (Princeton: Princeton University Press, 1960), pp. 8-14.

[8]Hoffmann, Contemporary Theory, pp. 30-37.

[9]I. L. Claude has demonstrated this ambiguity. Power and International Relations (New York: Random House, 1962), pp. 25-37.

[10]Hoffmann, Contemporary Theory, p. 30.

[11]Hans J. Morgenthau, "Wild Bunch," The New York Review of Books (February 11, 1971), p. 40.

[12]Hoffmann, Contemporary Theory, p. 35.

[13]The panel consisted of John C. Bennett, Richard Shaull, Alan Geyer, Tom F. Driver, Roger L. Shinn, Harvey G. Cox and Robert W. Lynn. Their discussion was published as "Christian Realism: Retrospect and Prospect," Christianity and Crisis (August 5, 1968), pp. 175-190.

CHAPTER VIII.   POWER AND PURPOSE

[1]Morgenthau, Politics Among Nations, p. 25.

[2]Ibid., p. 26.

[3]Paul Tillich, Love, Power and Justice (New York: Oxford University Press, 1954), p. 40.

[4]F. C. German, "A Tentative Evaluation of World Power," The Journal of Conflict Resolution (March, 1960).

[5]Ibid.

[6]The definition is from Professor W. T. R. Fox of Columbia University. A former student of Professor Fox, I am unable to claim that all the subtleties of his discussion of power are recognized here, nor do I now know if that definition is an exact quotation. However the relational-intentional emphasis of the concept is certainly Professor Fox's idea.

[7]The motifs discussed in this section are a modification of the Christ and culture motifs of H. Richard Niebuhr in Christ and Culture (New York: Harper and Bros., 1951).

[8]See Edward L. Long, Jr., A Survey of Christian Ethics (New York: Oxford University Press, 1967), p. vi.

[9]John C. Bennett, Foreign Policy in Christian Perspective (New York: Charles Scribner's Sons, 1966), p. 53.

CHAPTER IX. REVOLUTION: CONCEPTUAL ANALYSIS AND NORMS

[1]See William May, "The Mythic Foundations of the Politics of the Conservative," Soundings, LIII (Spring, 1970), pp. 20-45.

[2]Craine Brinton, The Anatomy of Revolution (New York: Vintage Book, 1965), p. 4.

[3]Carl J. Friedrich, ed., Revolution (New York: Atherton Press, 1967), p. 5.

[4]C. B. Macpherson in ibid., p. 140.

[5]Hannah Arendt, On Revolution (London: Faber and Faber, 1963), p. 27.

[6]Eugene Kamenka in Friedrich, ed., Revolution, p. 129.

[7]Ibid., p. 124.

[8]Paul Schrecker in ibid., p. 37.

[9]This diagram is a modified version of a design by Paul D. Ramshaw, whose paper on "Revolution" in a tutorial with the author is reflected in the above discussion.

[10]Edmund Burke, Reflections on the Revolution in France (Indianapolis: The Bobbs-Merrill Company, Inc., 1955), pp. 34-35.

[11]Cone, Black Theology and Black Power, p. 142.

[12]Moltmann, Religion, Revolution, and the Future, p. 144.

[13]Burke, Reflections on the Revolution in France, pp. 34-35.

[14]Maximilien Robespierre, "Speech on the Moral and Political Principles of Domestic Policy," Philip Dawson, ed., The French Revolution (Englewood Cliffs, N. J.: Prentice-Hall, Inc., 1967), p. 135.

[15]See Walter Wiest's perceptive critique of Paul Ramsey's arguments about violence in Christian ethics. "Can There Be a Christian Ethic of Violence?" Perspective, X (Fall, 1969), pp. 127-154.

CHAPTER X.   THE THEOLOGY OF LIBERATION

[1]Gustavo Gutierrez, A Theology of Liberation (Maryknoll: Orbis Books, 1973).

[2]Juan Luis Segundo, A Theology for Artisans of a New Humanity, I, II (Maryknoll: Orbis Books, 1973).

[3]G. Arevalo Catalino, Lecture at Tenth Theological Study Institute of Southeast Asian Theological Association, Singapore (August 1, 1972).

[4]Gutierrez, Theology, p. 236.

[5]Ibid., pp. 6-11.

[6]Ibid., p. 13.

[7]Quoted in ibid., p. 13.

[8]Ibid., p. 26.

[9]Ibid., p. 36.

[10]Ibid., p. 37.

[11]Nine pages plus eight pages of notes.

[12]Gutierrez, Theology, p. 119.

[13]Richard J. Neuhaus, "Liberation Theology and the Captivities of Jesus," Worldview, XVI (June, 1973), p. 48.

[14]Gutierrez, Theology, p. 298.

[15]Ibid., p. 103.

[16]Ibid., p. 231.

[17]Ibid., p. 232.

[18]Ibid., p. 236.

[19]Alves, Theology, pp. 11, 28, 84.

[20] Ibid., p. 39.

[21] Ibid., pp. 54-55.

[22] Ibid., p. 68.

[23] He attempts to further this internal dialogue in "Marxism as the Guarantee of Faith," _Worldview_, XVI (March, 1973), pp. 13-17.

[24] Alves, _Theology_, p. 105.

[25] Ibid., p. 109.

[26] Ibid.

[27] See Emilo Castro, "Uruguay: A Marxist Alleluia," and Renato Poblete, "Socialist and Christian in Chile," _Worldview_, XV (April, 1972), pp. 18-30.

[28] See Dom Helder Camara, "Principalities and Corporations," _Worldview_, XV (March, 1972), pp. 42-44.

CHAPTER XI.   THE KINGDOM OF GOD AND COUNTERREVOLUTION

[1] Norman Perrin, _Rediscovering the Teaching of Jesus_ (New York: Harper and Row, Publishers, 1967), p. 67.

[2] Dean Acheson, "Ethics in International Relations Today" in David L. Larson, _The Puritan Ethic in United States Foreign Policy_ (Princeton: D. Van Nostrand Co., Inc., 1966), pp. 131-144.

[3] Seymour Melman, _Pentagon Capitalism_ (New York: McGraw-Hill Book Company, 1970).

[4] Robert L. Heilbroner, "Making a Rational Foreign Policy Now," _Congressional Record_, 114 (September 18, 1968), p. E8057.

[5] The National Council of Churches, "Message to the Churches," May 20, 1970.

[6] Adolf A. Berle, _Latin America--Diplomacy and Reality_ (New York: Council on Foreign Relations, 1962). His study represents the ideology for the Alliance for Progress, and a perspective opposite to that presented here.

[7] Ernest W. Lefever, "America's Military Burden in the Third World," _Worldview_, XII (June, 1970), p. 13.

[8] William Appleman Williams, _The Tragedy of American Diplomacy_ (New York: Dell Publishing Co., 1962), p. 309.

[9] Matthew 25:45.

[10] Moltmann, _Religion, Revolution and the Future_, p. 217.